THE KEW GARDENER'S GUIDE TO

GROWING
SHRUBS

THE KEW GARDENER'S GUIDE TO

GROWING SHRUBS

THE ART AND SCIENCE TO
GROW YOUR OWN SHRUBS

VALERIE BOUJARD

FRANCES
LINCOLN

Contents

Introduction to growing shrubs

—

THE VALUE OF SHRUBS

Since the beginning of my career, first as a garden designer and now as a horticulturalist, I have planted and looked after hundreds of shrubs in many different gardens and various settings. Over the years, these versatile plants have become my garden best friends – and they will always be. They are, I believe, the most rewarding plants. I do not think I would be able to plant a garden without a shrub.

On account of the diversity of shrubs that can be grown nowadays, you can easily find a shrub for any and every situation. Whether it be for a large garden or a small balcony, a shady patio or a sunny border, in the city or in the countryside, you will undoubtedly encounter the shrub to fulfil your needs and expectations. These plants come in different sizes and shapes. Ground-cover shrubs fill up the front of a border and, in turn, reduce weeds. Tall upright ones bring height to a planting scheme. The shrubs at the back of a flower bed define the framework of a garden, and make a permanent background for the surrounding plants. When planted among perennials and other plants, shrubs bring permanence, structure, movement and contrast.

Depending on what they have to offer, shrubs can be planted individually in a border or in the middle of a lawn. They act as focal points as they become the centres of attention once they bloom (for example, common lilac/*Syringa vulgaris*), showcase their fiery autumn colours (spindle/*Euonymus europaeus* 'Red Cascade') or develop their attractive winter stems (dogwood/*Cornus sanguinea* 'Midwinter Fire'). When planted in large groups, shrubs create an instant impact in large landscaping projects (Wilson's honeysuckle/*Lonicera nitida*) or can be used to form hedges (garden privet/ *Ligustrum ovalifolium*).

Shrubs can be just right to block the view from a neighbour's window and give that much-needed privacy in urban areas. When planted against buildings and walls, they soften the structure and provide some colour. Certain shrubs act as windbreaks, offering shelter from coastal winds and salt sprays and protecting plants that are less resistant to wind. Hedging shrubs are a green, cost-effective alternative to brick walls or wooden fences, to mark the boundaries of a property. Not only do they provide protection, but, unlike landscaping materials, they also create a feeling of lushness: a more natural backdrop that reduces noise and pollution (see also Planting a hedge, page 126).

Although shrubs don't grow as tall as trees, they bring a welcome permanent structure to the garden.

All shrubs – and in particular hedging shrubs when they replace wooden fences or walls – are wonderful for wildlife. They offer food, protection and habitat. Birds will nest within their branches, and eat their berries in winter. Bees and butterflies will feast on the pollen of their flowers. Beetles, spiders and little mammals will find shelter under their foliage. Hedges provide food for us, too: berries for preserves; herbs for the kitchen; essential oils for fragrance and cosmetics; natural medicines; ingredients for drinks; and many other products for human consumption.

WHAT IS A SHRUB?

We often get confused when it comes to identifying a plant as a shrub. What is the difference between a small tree and a large shrub, between an evergreen perennial and an evergreen shrub? Is a plant that does not die back in winter always a shrub? It is difficult to draw a line between such plants. In fact, botanists, nursery staff, garden designers and horticulturalists do not share the same definition of a shrub.

To botanists, it means a plant with multiple woody stems growing at ground level or just above the ground with a few centimetres of trunk. These stems are permanent, and they do not die back to ground level in winter, like some perennials. Shrubs usually form branches, which grow bigger year after year and are sometimes up to 8m/26ft tall (some shrubs are 15m/50ft tall). They can be evergreen or deciduous and, when happy, they last for a long period of time. Large shrubs can be pruned to form small trees while shorter ones are often used to cover the ground and so are called subshrubs.

To nursery staff, shrubs are long-term garden plants. They are sold in containers in a range of different sizes – usually of 2, 5, 7.5, 10 or 15 litres. Some trees, like Japanese maple (*Acer palmatum*), are sold as shrubs in big pots of 20 litres. Shrubs are propagated by cuttings (softwood, semi-ripe, hardwood; see pages 31, 32 and 33, respectively).

To garden designers, a shrub is any hard-working, low-maintenance plant that can bring immediate impact and structure to a planting scheme. It is a plant, woody or not, with or without branches, that stays year-round, year after year. To them, shrubs are planted in large numbers to bring instant greenery in large landscaping projects, or individually as specimen plants or focal points. They are also chosen according to their shape and foliage, to bring height and contrast to the design. Thus, phormiums, yuccas, periwinkles (*Vinca*), pachysandras, spurges (*Euphorbia*) and grasses are considered shrubs by garden designers.

The professional horticulturalists exclude all those plants that are not true shrubs even though they are used as shrubs by the gardening industry. Thus, multi-stemmed trees such as Juneberry (*Amelanchier*) and woody or non-woody perennials such as phormiums or yuccas will not be mentioned in this book. Roses have their own book (*The Kew Gardener's Guide to Growing Roses*), while climbing shrubs could be the subject of another book in the series.

The shrubs described in this book are very easy to identify as shrubs, and they will do what shrubs do very well – bring

OPPOSITE TOP Shrubs are distinguished from trees by their multiple stems and shorter height.
OPPOSITE BOTTOM With their different shapes and foliages, shrubs add interest to the border.

There is a shrub for every situation, from a rock garden to a woodland setting. When an appropriate shrub is planted, it should then flourish.

a permanent structure to your garden or your patio, and also varied colours through their flowers, foliage and stems, year after year, provided they receive a reasonable amount of care.

SHRUBS IN THE GARDEN

Shrubs are long-term woody plants. Once planted and well established, they grow, flower, produce fruits and lose or keep their leaves, and the cycle continues year after year. They are relatively easy to look after. They don't need to be replanted, divided or replaced like perennials or bulbs. They are much more resistant to pest and diseases than vegetables. They don't need support like climbing plants.

Probably the only things you will have to do are pruning (see page 28) and feeding (see page 27) from time to time.

Shrubs provide year-round interest, too, and will have something to show. It can be their leaves if they are evergreen, or their autumn colours if they are deciduous. Some display attractive stems once the leaves have fallen; others bear berries on naked branches. Some shrubs flower in spring, while others do so in the middle of winter. Their flowers are very often beautifully scented. Satisfyingly, they don't die back like other plants at the end of the growing season; they are always there during the cold winter months as much as in the warm summer days.

Many shrubs grow well in pots and other types of container, and mix successfully with plants such as bulbs and perennials.

Their foliage comes in a variety of leaf shapes and colours – from the big broad leaves of Japanese aralia (*Fatsia japonica*), which will give you the kick-off for a jungle look (see Creating a jungle garden, page 72), to the tiny leaves of common box (*Buxus sempervirens*), which are appreciated for their density. The palette of colour is also noticeable, from the dark purple leaves of tawhiwhi (*Pittosporum tenuifolium* 'Tom Thumb') to the bright red foliage of Christmas berry (*Photinia* × *fraseri* 'Red Robin').

A well-thought-out mix of different shrubs with various sizes, forms, leaf shapes and colours will bring contrast and movement to the garden.

SHRUBS IN CONTAINERS

Shrubs grow very well in pots. It is worth trying to put your favourite shrub in a container if the soil in your garden is inappropriate. If you have no soil at all, put some pots on a balcony, fill them up with the right shrubs, and this tiny, otherwise unappealing space will become your very own natural paradise.

When walking through a city, I find myself observing the use of shrubs in vertical plantings, or so-called green walls. Plants such as Japanese aralia (*Fatsia japonica*) and sweet box (*Sarcococca confusa*) are now planted in bags among ferns and other evergreen perennials to cover large surfaces on building walls.

I have my doubts about the well-being of such large plants growing in such small bags, but only the future will tell if this new trend will be sustainable or not for shrubs. See also Growing a shrub in a container, page 96.

WHAT SHRUBS CAN YOU GROW AND WHERE?

As we have seen, shrubs come in all sizes, foliage colours, leaf shapes, deciduous or evergreen. They can be grown for their flowers or just for their stems. The variety of plants available has never been so rich. No matter the size of your space, large or small, the location, if rural or urban, and whether it's a garden or a terrace, there is a shrub for every situation, which can transform your space into a beautiful patch of nature. Therefore, you can easily

get lost and confused when it comes to choosing a shrub.

Before buying, you must check the soil in your garden. Some shrubs – for example, lavender (*Lavandula*), rock rose (*Cistus*) and cotton lavender (*Santolina*) – thrive in very poor soils, and others need fertile, humus-rich ones. Shrubs such as camellias or rhododendrons need acidic soil; others require moist ground. If possible, have a look at the surrounding vegetation, which will give you some precious information about the type of soil in your garden. Otherwise do a soil test with a kit bought from a garden centre.

Then, assess how much sun or shade there is in the area where you want to plant

Before buying a shrub for your border, make sure that it will have enough space to grow freely to its mature size.

your shrub. There are shrubs for full sun, and those whose leaves burn if they are not planted in shade. Pay attention to the surrounding trees as they can create a lot of shade once in full leaf.

Is it very windy where you live? Some shrubs such as New Zealand broadleaf (*Griselinia littoralis*) are great windbreakers. Not only will they grow happily in exposed conditions but they will also protect the other plants from cold and drying winds.

Is it very cold? Hardiness is an important factor in growing a shrub successfully. Once they are in the ground you will not be able to bring your shrub indoors for winter protection. It is, therefore, essential to choose a shrub that will be able to cope with the coolest temperatures in your area. If you want to grow a plant that is not completely hardy, it is possible to cover it with horticultural fleece during the coldest months. I have done this with a tea tree (*Leptospermum scoparium*) in London, and it worked very well. Another good option is to plant your favourite shrub in a container (see Growing a shrub in a container, page 96) and bring the pot into a greenhouse or other shelter, to protect it from frosts.

Another important consideration when deciding what to grow is the annual rainfall in your area. However, with a fast-changing climate, the weather becomes more and more unpredictable. Although plants have to adapt, some are now struggling, even dying during the dry summer months. Irrigation is not the best solution as it is not sustainable, and many regions are now implementing

---

Hardiness ratings

In this book, the tenderest shrubs (*Coprosma repens* and *Melianthus major*) are classified H3 and the hardiest ones (*Berberis thunbergii* and *Cotoneaster horizontalis*) are classified H7. The vast majority are between H4 and H6.

H3: the plant tolerates temperatures of –5°C/23°F to 1°C/34°F. It is considered half-hardy and can grow outside in regions with mild winters.
H4: the plant tolerates temperatures of –10°C/14°F to –5°C/23°F. It is considered hardy and does well in temperate regions. It may suffer during harsh weather in winter if planted in a cold garden.

H5: the plant tolerates temperatures of –15°C/5°F to –10°C/14°F. It is hardy and can withstand cold winters and brief episodes of frosts.
H6: the plant tolerates temperatures of –20°C/–4°F to –15°C/5°F. It is hardy and grows well in very cold winters and can cope with long episodes of severe frosts.
H7: the plant tolerates temperatures colder than –20°C/–4°F. It is considered very hardy and does not suffer during extreme cold conditions, even in exposed locations.

hosepipe bans in summer. The gardening trend should be to move towards more and more drought-resistant plants such as Mediterranean shrubs – for example, lavender (*Lavandula*), myrtle (*Myrtus*) and helichrysum.

Finally, how much space do you have for gardening? It is very important to ensure you have room for the shrub once it matures. A little shrub, 30cm/12in wide and tall in a nursery, will become a much bigger plant after some years in your garden. Therefore, always consider the shrub's mature height. It is worth spending time on drawing a planting plan to scale. A rough sketch on which you can draw little circles representing each shrub once mature will suffice; it need not be too complicated but will give you a very good indication of how the area might be filled.

WHAT DO YOU WANT FROM YOUR SHRUB?

Once you have assessed your soil, wind exposure and planting space, you need to decide what you want to get from your shrub. How do you want to use it? Is it to be a focal point in the middle of the lawn, a gap filler in the border, or a boundary plant for your property? Do you want an evergreen shrub that will bring a permanent structure to your border, just by offering constant green foliage year-round? Do you prefer a deciduous shrub that may not do that much in winter but will display amazing autumn colours? Are you looking for beautiful flowers and lovely scents? Flowering shrubs make

wonderful specimens when in full bloom. Think about the joy of common lilac (*Syringa vulgaris*) flowers, camellias or Californian lilac (*Ceanothus*). Even though some flowers do not last very long, they are such a delight when they do explode with their various colours and sometimes delicate fragrances. Lastly, would you rather help our fragile wildlife by choosing a shrub that will give insects and birds plenty of pollen and berries to feast on?

Once you have an idea of what type of shrub you want, there are still a few more things to consider before making a final selection. Think about how your shrub is going to work with your existing planting, bearing in mind that once your shrub is in the ground it will be difficult to move it. As it will stay in that spot for many many years, it is critical to take as much time as needed when it comes to choosing the right shrub.

If you want to plant your shrub in a container, select one that grows comfortably in a pot, and remember that a container-grown shrub needs more watering and feeding than one planted in the ground (see Aftercare: Looking after shrubs in containers, page 25).

SHRUBS FOR HEDGES

Hedges are wonderful to mark the boundary of your garden, to provide some privacy and protection from noise and pollution, and to offer habitat, food and shelter for wildlife. You can plant a hedge to divide areas of your garden, to hide an unsightly wall or to protect yourself or your plants from wind.

Traditional hedges are formal and dense. They are planted with evergreen shrubs such as garden privet (*Ligustrum ovalifolium*), tawhiwhi (*Pittosporum*

OPPOSITE TOP AND BOTTOM Some shrubs such as dogwood (*Cornus*) are grown for their colourful stems, while others such as lilac (*Syringa*) are treasured for their beautiful scented blooms.

When grown as a hedge, a shrub will bring you privacy as well as reduce noise and pollution.

tenuifolium) or New Zealand broadleaf (*Griselinia littoralis*) and are usually sold by hedge specialists, which offer plants sufficiently large to create a boundary with immediate impact.

Flowering hedges are free-growing and colourful, and can be of a single genus (firethorn/*Pyracantha*, for example) or be a mix of different genera (barberry/*Berberis*, spiraea and forsythia, for example). Specialized nurseries give good advice on how to choose the right flowering hedge for your garden.

Low-growing hedges are neat, compact and 0.5–1.5m/1½–5ft tall. They are great for creating patterns and divisions without obscuring a view. Box (*Buxus*) is the all-star plant for a low hedge, even though it can be decimated by box blight (see page 133) and box tree caterpillars (see page 132). It is often replaced by Japanese holly (*Ilex crenata*). Lavender (*Lavandula*) and rosemary (*Salvia rosmarinus*) also make wonderful and colourful low hedges.

You can purchase ready-made hedging plants online, especially via nurseries that specialize in hedges. Before you buy, it is important to get the planting distance between each shrub right, as you don't want to plant too densely or too sparsely. Such advice should be given on the nursery's website. As a rule, the standard planting distance is 3–5 plants per metre/yard for plants that are sold in 2-litre pots, and three

Before purchasing a shrub always check that its branches and leaves look attractive and healthy and that the shrub is not root-bound.

plants per metre/yard for plants sold in 5-litre pots.

Pot-grown plants are available year-round, while bare-root hedging shrubs are available from late autumn until mid-spring. These are cheaper than pot-grown plants, but you will need 5–7 plants per metre/yard. See also Planting a hedge, page 126.

CHOOSING AND BUYING

The most common place to go to buy a shrub is a local garden centre or nursery. Wandering around the wide selection of plants there is one of the first joys of your garden project. You will find shrubs that have proven to grow well in your area,

and, as they will be displayed outdoors, they are already accustomed to the local weather and temperatures.

Once in the garden centre, it should be easy to locate the shrubs, as they are very often arranged by seasonal interest. You may find a section with autumn-berried shrubs if you visit in autumn or with spring-flowering shrubs if you go in spring. Consider the size of the shrub and the pot straight away. A plant in a 10-litre pot may be difficult to carry, while a very tall shrub may not fit in your vehicle. Then check that the leaves are nice and healthy; look carefully (underneath) for signs of pests and diseases. Stems should be without breaks or any other damage.

Stand back and look for a plant with a well-balanced appearance. The soil in the pot should be free from weeds and moss. Finally, check the roots by looking at the bottom of the pot. If roots are showing, it means that the shrub has been in the container for too long and may have suffered some lack of nutrients. Exposed roots on the surface are another sign of starvation. Some people like to take the shrub out of its pot to see the state of the root ball, but I do not recommend doing this as any resulting damage would upset the seller. Remember your shrub doesn't have to be particularly large or expensive. Some shrubs are fast growing and will do wonderfully in no time, saving you money. Smaller shrubs are also easier to establish in their new home.

With more and more in-person restrictions, busier lives and worsening traffic jams, you may want to consider buying your shrub online. It will certainly save you a lot of time and you don't need a vehicle. Online nurseries are invading the web. Read the customers reviews carefully and choose the nursery that is a registered business and that sells plants with passports. Any plants entering the UK, for example, should have been checked for pests and diseases before being issued with a passport.

The plant you want to buy will usually come with amazing photos. However, the one that will arrive at your door can look very different from the one you expected. Most of the time this doesn't really matter as your plant – if not badly damaged – will, with time, grow well in your garden.

Shipping times can be very long, so pay attention to those when making your purchase. Also, plants can be damaged during shipment; no matter how much packaging has been used, there is always a risk.

WHEN TO PLANT YOUR SHRUB

Once you have bought your shrub, try to plant it as soon as you can. However, plants sold in pots can stay for a little while longer in their containers, provided that you give them enough water, air and light during their time before planting.

In temperate regions, you can plant shrubs year-round as long as the ground is not frozen. However, spring and autumn are the optimum planting times, because the shrub can establish before the dry summer weather or the cold winter months. Your shrub will hopefully receive rainwater during these periods, which is a real advantage. Rainwater is always better for plants than tap water, and is certainly much more sustainable.

Some shrubs, such as small evergreen ones, are sold root-balled, that is, with a fabric mesh (hessian) tightly wrapped around each root ball. They are available in autumn and spring, when planting conditions are ideal, and can be left unplanted for a little while, provided that each root ball is kept moist.

Some deciduous shrubs are sold bare-root. These are sent via the post or courier during the winter months, when the plants are dormant. On arrival, put bare-root shrubs in a bucket of water until they can be planted. They should be put in the ground as soon as possible as they don't have any nutrients to rely on.

Carefully firm the soil around your shrub after you have planted it, so that you remove any air pockets.

EQUIPMENT

You should be able to use general gardening tools when planting shrubs, the essentials for which are listed below. Make sure that the tools are clean before using them. This will help to reduce the spread of diseases.

- a fork and a spade for digging the hole the shrub will go in;
- a hand trowel and a hand fork for weeding; it can also be used for digging if your shrub is very small;
- a half-moon edger if you plant your shrub in the lawn;
- a pair of gardening gloves for protection against spiky shrubs such as firethorn (*Pyracantha*);
- a kneeler for comfort, especially if the ground is wet and muddy;
- a watering can or a hosepipe for watering;
- a bucket of water for keeping bare-root plants moist.

Pruning equipment
- secateurs for stems thinner than 1cm/½in;
- long-handled pruners for thicker stems, and for reaching tall shrubs;
- pruning saw for big branches;
- garden shears for trimming leaves on hedges or formal shapes such as topiary.

Well-cleaned, very sharp tools are essential when it comes to pruning your plant. Always disinfect the blade between pruning each shrub, to minimize the risk of spreading infection.

POTTING SOILS AND COMPOSTS

Most shrubs do well in a wide variety of soils as long as the ground is well-drained. Heavy clay is and will always be a problem, even with the constant addition of clay breakers such as spent mushroom compost. Acid-loving shrubs such as pieris, rhododendron and camellia must be planted in acidic soil. If you are not sure about the pH, mix half of your existing soil with the same amount of ericaceous compost, in the planting hole. If your acid-loving shrub is to go into a pot, fill the container with ericaceous potting compost. Because sandy soils are required for shrubs that need poor soil and excellent drainage, my advice would be to make a mix of two parts topsoil, one part horticultural sand and one part horticultural grit, and fill up the hole or your container with that mix. All other shrubs need only good-quality multipurpose potting compost if grown in containers, or your ordinary garden soil if planted in a border (see Planting a pot-grown shrub in the ground, page 104).

Compost or growing media for plant cuttings
Cuttings will start rooting best in a soilless media such as perlite, vermiculite, sand or a mixture of these three. You can also find ready-made cutting composts in any good garden centre or online. Such loose, well-drained mixtures will provide plenty of oxygen for the new roots to develop. They are also low in nutrients as young plants are not greedy at this stage of development. See also Propagation, page 31.

Some simple tips when planting shrubs

- Choose the right shrub for the right place – the soil, the amount of moisture in it, light levels, temperatures and other climatic conditions such as wind or frost have to suit the new plant.
- Buy a vigorous plant with a well-formed root ball and healthy-looking leaves and branches.
- Take your time when planting by preparing the ground, planting at the right depth (see Planting a pot-grown shrub in the ground, page 104), and firming the soil around the shrub.
- Water generously after planting and regularly afterwards until the shrub is well established. During periods of drought, don't let the soil dry out.
- Check the water drainage regularly – saturated water can be fatal for your plant (see Automatic watering systems, page 24).
- Protect your shrub from frost and snow with horticultural fleece wrapped around the foliage, or a 10–15cm/4–6in layer of mulch or straw around the base of the plant; move container-grown tender shrubs indoors or into a greenhouse, if possible.
- Watch out for any pests and diseases – early detection of potential problems means they are easier to control (see Troubleshooting, page 130).

AFTERCARE

Although shrubs are considered low-maintenance plants, they still require care over the years to maintain good health and to promote new growth.

Watering

During their first year, your shrubs need regular watering. Keep an eye on the soil and do not let it dry out. A good soak once a week is better than scant watering every day. You may have to water every other day during hot dry periods in summer. Once each shrub is established, water only at the first sign of thirst (dry soil, wilted leaves). See also Automatic watering systems, below.

Mulching

Mulch can be an organic material of decomposed garden compost, farmyard manure, or wood and bark from shredded trees. Pine needles for acid-loving plants

---

Automatic watering systems

Automatic irrigation systems can do more harm than good. When they are poorly regulated, they are very often responsible for waterlogged soils. How many times have I observed plants sitting in puddles with sprinklers still on, or sprinklers on even on rainy days? Irrigation systems should be used wisely, and turned off in wet weather. Position sprinklers in such a way that the jets of water reach the soil without touching the plant foliage.

---

or straw for less hardy ones can also be very useful. Applying a mulch, 10–15cm/4–6in deep, brings many benefits to your plants.

- It retains soil moisture, which helps to minimize the need for additional watering. Evaporation is also reduced due to the thick layer of decomposed matter. Thus, mulching has now become more and more essential with our longer periods of drought.
- It protects plant roots from cold weather and frost by creating a blanket to preserve warmth in the soil.
- It reduces weeds by stopping the sunlight that allows weeds to germinate and deprives them of soil. Weeds are not only unsightly, but they also compete with shrubs for nutrients.
- It minimizes erosion by protecting the soil from getting swept away by heavy downpours.
- It feeds the soil by naturally breaking down organic material and releasing nutrients into the soil. A healthy soil full of worms and micro-organisms is essential for plants to perform year after year.
- It creates healthy soils; this in turn encourages healthy shrubs, which are less prone to pests and diseases.
- It ensures a border or planting space looks neat when covered in a fresh layer of mulch.

Mulching can be done before the first cold weather in autumn, when the soil is moist and still warm – and not yet frozen. In summer, mulch to prevent the soil drying out during extended periods of drought. Make sure that all mulching material is well decomposed before using

Mulch will not only protect your plant from frost, but also help to retain moisture during the driest months.

it, otherwise it may rot and cause more damage than good. When applying mulch around your shrubs, leave space around the woody stems so that the mulch doesn't touch them.

Winter protection

Some half-hardy shrubs may need winter protection in cold areas (see Hardiness ratings, page 15) or if heavy snow or a severe winter temperatures occur. Just before the first signs of frost, wrap your shrub in horticultural fleece (available in garden centres and DIY stores) and secure it with string. This will bring extra protection and may save your plant from dying of cold.

Looking after shrubs in containers

These need more care than those grown in the ground since their restricted space doesn't give them natural access to water and nutrients. Thus, they should have regular watering throughout their lifespans, and the potting compost should be changed every year until they are well established, to give plants the essential nutrients they need to perform optimally.

Containers need appropriate watering – not too much and not too little. You don't want saturated soil, but you don't want the soil to dry out either. For a large pot, a full watering can once a week should suffice. Always keep an eye on the soil moisture, even if it is raining because

rainwater doesn't always reach into the pot. Water more, possibly every day, during hot and dry weather.

Every year in spring, replace the top 10cm/4in of soil with new potting compost mixed withg controlled-release fertilizer. Be careful not to damage the roots.

Once the plant is well established, replace the top layer of soil with organic farmyard manure. Then cover with a woody mulch or horticultural grit, to retain the moisture and limit weed growth. Because nutrients quickly run low in pots, feed your shrub twice a year with controlled-release fertilizer (see Applying fertilizers, below).

A frost-resistant container is highly recommended during the cold months, but if you don't have one you can always protect your container with bubble wrap. Tender plants can be moved indoors during the winter months.

Removing suckers

Shrubs that are grafted on to a rootstock often produce suckers that can become a real nuisance in your border. These unwanted shoots from below the ground should be removed as soon as they appear and as close as possible to the point of origin on the root. Carefully scrap away the soil to reach the base of the sucker and tear it away; in this way, you will also remove the dormant buds. If tearing is not possible, cut the sucker with sharp clean secateurs, as close as possible to its base.

Don't forget to mulch your potted plants because it will help the soil from drying out fast, regulate the soil temperature, and protect the roots from the sun.

Applying fertilizers

In most cases, applying mulch (see Mulching, page 24) regularly around your shrub will give it all the nutrients it needs. The three essential nutrients for shrubs are nitrogen (for growth and healthy green leaves), potassium (for healthy roots and flower growth) and phosphorus (for development and protection from pests and diseases).

Shrubs sometimes require micronutrients such as magnesium (to give leaves their green colour) or iron (for the production of chlorophyll through photosynthesis). Iron also plays a role in the production of energy and in the transport of nutrients throughout the plant's tissues. Signs of magnesium deficiency appear on older leaves first, as they become yellow between the veins and around the edges. Other colours such as purple or brown might also appear. Symptoms of iron deficiency appear on the newer leaves first. They turn yellow while the veins stay green for a while. See also Nutrient deficiency, page 137.

Fertilizers are necessary only if your shrubs show signs of nutrient deficiency such as slow growth, discoloured or smaller leaves than normal or poor blooms. A general balanced fertilizer can then be applied. The best time to apply fertilizer is either just before or just after the growing season. Spring fertilization encourages new vigorous growth, while autumn feeding gives roots a boost of nutrients before the cold winter months.

Controlled-release fertilizers or granular ones will provide nutrition throughout the growing season by releasing their nutrients over time. They are easy to apply and well suited to young shrubs. For a quicker boost of nutrients, use fast-release fertilizers or

When done correctly and at the right time, pruning will encourage more blooms the following year.

water-soluble ones, but they can leach more quickly through the soil without benefiting the shrub's roots.

You can also make your own liquid feed from nettles or comfrey – the method is the same for both plants (see Making organic nettle-tea fertilizer, page 64).

PRUNING

Pruning can be confusing, especially regarding shrubs. Some shrubs need only very little pruning or no pruning at all, while others require cutting every year. Hard pruning (see page 30) is sometimes necessary to restore an overgrown shrub.

There is a tool for nearly every branch size (see Pruning equipment, page 22).

Each tool should be kept clean and well sharpened, so all cuts are neat – and never jagged.

For many shrubs, the sole reason to prune is to remove old, dead, damaged or crossing branches, as well as stems that spoil the symmetry of the plant. However, for shrubs that produce flowers, pruning encourages the development of new flowering shoots and, therefore, more beautiful blooms the following year.

If done properly, pruning will help maintain the health and beauty of your shrub, but if done badly or incorrectly it can cause serious damage (see Physical damage, page 137).

Evergreen shrubs can be pruned to control their size and shape. For all but flowering evergreens, this is generally done when they are dormant,.

Flowering shrubs

For the first two to three years after planting a shrub, let it fill out and don't prune it. This will help it to establish a good root system. Thereafter, its time of flowering will dictate when to prune.

Shrubs that bloom in summer or autumn, having formed their flower buds on new wood (the current year's growth), should be pruned in late winter and early spring so new stems grow soon after. This is the case for abelia, butterfly bush (*Buddleja*), hydrangea and St John's wort (*Hypericum*).

Spring-flowering shrubs, which produce blooms on growth from the previous year, need to be pruned just after flowering, once the blooms have faded. This gives the plant enough time to put on new growth and develop flower buds. Prune forsythia, deutzia and mock orange (*Philadelphus*) in this way.

Winter-flowering shrubs such as sweet box (*Sarcococca*) should be pruned right after flowering but before new buds start emerging, usually in late winter.

Evergreen shrubs

These are usually pruned for aesthetic purposes, to keep an open attractive appearance or for space requirements when they become too big and are disturbing the neighbouring plants by not allowing them to develop fully.

Hedging shrubs are usually clipped twice a year, or more often, to maintain their neat appearance and to encourage dense growth.

When removing unwanted branches, cut them right back to the base. Add a 10–15cm/4–6in layer of organic farmyard manure afterwards.

The best time to prune most evergreen shrubs is late winter or early spring, when they are dormant. However, an evergreen flowering shrub should be pruned just after flowering, once the flowers have faded.

Hard pruning

Most overgrown deciduous shrubs that have been neglected for many years and have become too dense, too big and too crowded can be pruned drastically by removing all stems down to near ground level, leaving stems just 10–15cm/4–6in long above the ground. Butterfly bush (*Buddleja*) responds very well to such pruning (see Rejuvenating a butterfly bush, page 42).

Deciduous shrubs that do not respond well to such drastic, one-off pruning should be cut back over two years. Remove half the branches at ground level the first winter, starting with the oldest wood. Then the following winter, cut the remaining old stems back to ground level. For more sensitive plants, do such pruning over three seasons, by cutting only one-third of the old stems each winter.

Evergreen shrubs are much more sensitive to hard pruning and very often cannot be renovated. It is possible to try pruning them hard, but if this doesn't bring satisfactory results the shrub will have to be replaced.

After pruning, always apply a 10–15cm/4–6in layer of organic farmyard manure. This helps the plant to recover from the stress of hard pruning.

Hedge pruning

Hedges are an important habitat for wildlife and especially nesting birds, so always check for nests before trimming a hedge.

Deciduous hedges are pruned in the second year after planting. Between autumn and late winter, shorten the main stem and side branches by one-third, to just above a healthy bud. In the third and fourth year after planting, shorten only the new growth by one-third, just above a healthy bud. Thereafter, in early summer and again in winter, shorten the sides to form the permanent framework of your hedge.

Evergreen hedges should be pruned in spring, in the second year after planting, by shortening all branches by one-third. In the third and fourth year after planting, in summer, lightly prune any side branches. Then in the following early spring, prune harder to start shaping your hedge. Thereafter, keep trimming twice a year, to maintain the desired shape.

Wait until the flowers have died down to prune established flowering hedges. This will encourage even stronger blossom the following spring. See individual shrub profiles, pages 36–129 for more specific pruning advice on flowering shrubs.

Established deciduous and evergreen hedges need regular pruning to maintain their neat shapes and dense growth. You may need the help of a string line to obtain a straight cut all along your hedge.

Specific pruning is required for lavenders (*Lavandula*), hydrangeas and box (*Buxus*). See the relevant individual shrub profiles, pages 36–129.

PROPAGATION

There is nothing more satisfying than increasing your own stock of plants, and, fortunately, most shrubs can be propagated easily. Taking stem cuttings or layering for some specific shrubs is simple and very often will give successful results. Having your own little nursery allows you not only to increase the stock of your favourite shrub for your garden but also to create gifts from your very own plants for family and friends.

Softwood cuttings

Softwood cuttings have the highest rooting potential of any type of cutting material, and they are a good way to propagate many deciduous shrubs such as tree mallow (*Malva*), salvias (aka *Perovskia*) and hydrangeas. Take cuttings in spring or early summer, preferably in the morning, when the stems are full of water – softwood cuttings wilt quickly if they don't stay humid.

Before taking any cuttings, fill a container with cutting compost (see Compost or growing media for plant cuttings, page 23). Then venture into the garden to cut off some non-flowering stems, each with 3–5 pairs of leaves. Immediately place them in a plastic bag and seal it, to trap the moisture.

Once back in the house or shed, use a sharp knife to reduce each stem to 7–10cm/3–4in long by slicing it just below a leaf joint. Remove all but the uppermost four single (or two pairs) of leaves, and then dip the basal cut in a powder fungicide. Using a pencil or wooden stick, make a hole in the cutting compost and insert a cutting up to its leaves. Repeat for the other cuttings – you can have three or four cuttings per container, provided that the leaves do not touch each other.

Label the cuttings, and water the compost from above. Then place the container in a well-lit, protected area, ideally in a propagator with a bottom heat of 18–24°C/64–75°F. If you don't have a propagator, cover the pot with a plastic bag and seal it with an elastic band, then place it somewhere warm; remove the bag twice a week to ventilate the cuttings.

Once they have rooted, harden off the cuttings gradually (see Hardening off, below). Transplant them into individual pots. Having watered and labelled them, set them in a shady position until they are well established.

Semi-ripe cuttings

Semi-ripe cuttings are thicker and harder than softwood cuttings and, therefore, are more capable of survival. They are a good way to propagate many evergreen shrubs such as Mexican orange blossom (*Choisya*), Californian lilac (*Ceanothus*), fatsia or viburnum. They are also suitable for hedging plants such as box (*Buxus*), honeysuckle (*Lonicera*) and privet (*Ligustrum*).

Take semi-ripe cuttings in late summer until mid-autumn, when growth slows down and plant stems become woodier. The base of each cutting should be hard, while the tip of the stem is still soft.

Start by filling pots or a cold frame (in a warm, well-lit area) with a potting compost made of equal parts free-draining potting compost and perlite or sharp sand. With secateurs, cut off several shoots, each with all its current season's growth and immediately place each cutting in a plastic bag.

Trim off the soft tip of each cutting and remove the lowest pairs of leaves.

Hardening off

Before your cuttings can be moved out into the garden, they need hardening off. This process of getting them used to outdoor conditions should be done gradually over a period of two to three weeks. During that time, slowly increase airflow, day by day, by opening the lid of a cold frame. If you don't have a cold frame, place the plants in a sheltered spot in front of a warm wall and cover them with horticultural fleece to protect them from sun scorch and sudden changes of temperature. Leave the cuttings outside first for a couple of hours during the day, then for a longer period to acclimatize them to outdoor light levels and temperatures. In this way, your cuttings will be fully ready to deal with the environmental conditions of the outside world.

OPPOSITE TOP AND BOTTOM Semi-ripe cuttings (here of sage/*Salvia* and box/*Buxus sempervirens*) are taken between late summer and mid-autumn, and are an easy way to obtain new plants.

Once transplanted into their individual pots, semi-ripe cuttings will need regular watering to ensure their compost does not dry out.

With large-leaved plants reduce the size of the remaining leaves by about a half, to minimize water loss. Using a sharp knife, wound the stem by cutting away a piece of bark 2.5–4cm/1–1½in long from one side of its base, and then dip the wounded basal cut into hormone rooting powder. Make a hole in the pot or cold-frame compost with a pencil or wooden stick and insert the base of one cutting 4–6cm/ 1½–2½in deep into the compost, then plant the remaining cuttings 7–10cm/3–4in apart, making sure that their leaves do not touch each other.

Label and water thoroughly. Place any pots in a warm, well-lit area in a greenhouse or cover them with a plastic bag and seal each with an elastic band.

Once the cuttings are well-rooted, with roots 3–5cm/1¼–2in long, lift the new plants and pot them up individually. Harden them off gradually (see Hardening off, page 32) before transplanting them.

Hardwood cuttings
An easy way to propagate many deciduous shrubs and some evergreen ones is from hardwood cuttings. Forsythia, mock orange (*Philadelphus*) and elder (*Sambucus*) can be propagated by this method, as can evergreens such as privet (*Ligustrum*) and skimmia. Take hardwood cutting during the

dormant season, from late autumn (just after leaf fall) to late winter (just before the leaf buds break in spring).

Start by filling deep containers or a cold frame with a gritty potting compost comprising equal parts grit and multipurpose compost. Alternatively, propagate your hardwood cuttings in a sheltered bed or border, in well-drained soil.

Then cut strong healthy hardwood stems from this year's growth. Remove the soft tip and any leaves from each stem. Divide the stems into sections, each 15–20cm/6–8in long, making a clean sloping cut at the top, just above a bud or pair of buds. Make a horizontal cut at the base of each cutting, just below a bud or pair of buds. Then dip each basal end (with the horizontal cut) into hormone rooting powder and insert it into the prepared potting mix, leaving 2.5–5cm/1–2in of the cutting above ground. Insert the remaining cuttings 10cm/4in apart if in a container, or 15cm/6in apart if in an outdoor trench in a cold frame or border. Firm back the soil. Label the hardwood cuttings and, if in a container, place them in a sheltered cold frame or unheated greenhouse until the following autumn. Harden them off (see Hardening off, page 32) before transplanting outdoors (see Softwood cuttings, page 32).

Simple layering

This is a fun and easy method of propagating shrubs with flexible stems that are easy to bend down to ground level. For example, deciduous shrubs such as smoke tree (*Cotinus*) and flowering quince (*Chaenomeles*) respond better to propagation by layering than by stem cuttings, as do evergreens such as camellia, daphne and viburnum. The optimum time to layer deciduous shrubs is in autumn or spring, while evergreen ones are better layered in spring.

Choose a healthy, vigorous, young stem to be layered and bend it down to ground level. Using a stick, mark the point where the stem touches the soil. Dig a trench, 10–15cm/4–6in deep, from that point, making one side straight and sloping the other towards the parent plant. Bend the stem to be layered along the sloping side in the trench and peg it upright against the straight side, with only 1–2cm/½–¾in of stem and the top leaves showing above ground. Fill up the trench with soil, firm in and water well. Keep the soil moist, especially in dry weather.

Roots should develop within twelve months. Once a good root system has formed, sever the layered stem from its parent plant and replant in the open ground or in a pot. Leave to establish.

Plants

—

Abelia

Abelia × grandiflora

For a shrub that is loved by bees and perfect for cottage-style gardens, opt for this vigorous, low-maintenance, medium-sized abelia with its arching stems and glossy, semi-evergreen leaves. It flowers abundantly all summer until autumn, leaving a light fragrance in the air. In autumn, its foliage turns purple-bronze.

—

WHERE TO GROW

Abelias are not fully hardy. It thrives in well-drained, fertile soil in the shelter of another shrub, or when planted against a wall in full sun.

HOW TO GROW

In mid-spring, cut back some older stems by two-thirds or more to maintain the plant's graceful shape. At the same time remove any dead or damaged wood. Propagate by taking softwood cuttings (see page 31) or semi-ripe cuttings (see page 32).

GROWING TIP

Deadhead regularly to prolong flowering.

Family	Caprifoliaceae
Height and spread	2.5–4x2.5–4m/ 8–13x8–13ft
Habit	Rounded
Flowering time	Summer–autumn
Hardiness	H5
Position	Full sun

NOTABLE CULTIVAR

- 'Kaleidoscope' is a variegated dwarf shrub with lime-green foliage in spring, yellow in summer, then glossy orange and deep red leaves in autumn.

THE BEST OF EACH

A. × grandiflora is the result of a cross between *A. chinensis* (native to temperate China) and *A. uniflora* (originating from eastern China).

Japanese laurel

Aucuba japonica

Although they are too often relegated to unloved industrial areas, Japanese laurels are, in fact, excellent evergreen shrubs especially for harsh conditions such as dense shade. They present a luxurious, dark green foliage with glossy oval leaves. Female plants produce attractive, cylindrical, red berries if a male is growing nearby. These berries are a delight for birds.

WHERE TO GROW

Plant in any soil and any situation except very dry conditions. Japanese laurels tolerate pollution, sea spray and heatwaves.

HOW TO GROW

Being remarkably disease resistant and easy to care for, Japanese laurels need regular watering only in summer for the first two years. Once established, these shrubs tolerate short periods of drought. Propagate by taking semi-ripe cuttings (see page 32).

GROWING TIP

Pruning is not necessary but can be done in spring, to keep a bushy shape. Apply a 10–15cm/4–6in layer of garden compost or manure around the base of the plant afterwards.

Family Garryaceae

Height and spread 2.5–4x2.5–4m/ 8–13x8–13ft

Habit Rounded

Flowering time Spring

Hardiness H5

Position Full sun– full shade

NOTABLE CULTIVARS

- f. *longifolia* 'Salicifolia' develops deep green, narrow leaves on green stems and bright red berries if a male is nearby.
- 'Rozannie' is compact, with very glossy, dark green leaves and both male and female flowers, so produces bright red berries in summer and autumn.

TOO MUCH HATE

Aucuba japonica is too often associated with motorway service areas or creepy abandoned flower beds in business parks. It is not always treated fairly and certainly doesn't receive enough gratitude for the role it plays.

Barberry

Berberis thunbergii

This small to medium-sized deciduous shrub bears thorny stems and dark purple leaves that turn red and orange in autumn. Its pale yellow flowers are dotted with red, and are followed by little, rounded, red berries in autumn.

—

WHERE TO GROW

Plant in moist yet well-drained soil in full sun or partial shade. Barberry is an ideal shrub for a low hedge, such as a wildlife-friendly hedgerow (see Planting a hedge, page 126). It can also be clipped to create a more formal look or be planted in a container on a terrace or a balcony (see Growing a shrub in a container, page 96).

HOW TO GROW

When planting, dig a hole twice the size of the nursery pot, then insert the plant and backfill with a mixture of one part garden compost to every two parts soil. Water well afterwards. Prune lightly after flowering, by removing any dead, diseased or damaged stems. Propagate by seed or by taking semi-ripe cuttings (see page 32).

GROWING TIP

Between mid-spring and mid-autumn, keep an eye out for sawfly caterpillars (*see* Sawfly larvae, page 130) and handpick these off the plant as soon as spotted.

Family Berberidaceae	
Height and spread 1–1.5x1–1.5m/3–5x3–5ft	
Habit Compact	
Flowering time Spring	
Hardiness H7	
Position Sun–partial shade	

ANOTHER NOTABLE SPECIES

• *B. darwinii* is a fast-growing, evergreen shrub often used for hedging; it has delicate, dark green, holly-like, tiny leaves and masses of orange-yellow flowers in spring followed by purple-black berries. It often offers a second bloom in autumn; this is a little less abundant.

KEEP OFF
Thanks to its thorns, barberry makes an excellent defensive hedge.

Brachyglottis 'Sunshine'

Brachyglottis (Dunedin Group) 'Sunshine' aka *Senecio* 'Sunshine'

Beautiful, silver-grey foliage and a multitude of golden yellow, daisy-like flowers are the selling points of this small evergreen shrub, which is a cross between three species of *Brachyglottis*. It is certainly one of the most popular cultivars for temperate regions.

—

WHERE TO GROW

A very well-drained soil mix of two parts soil to one part grit or horticultural sand is essential, as is a warm sheltered position in full sun. Brachyglottis is a very good shrub for a coastal garden, dry soil or a container (see Growing a shrub in a container, page 96).

HOW TO GROW

Although easy to grow, it needs regular watering until it gets established. A light pruning after flowering will keep the shrub bushy and in good shape.

GROWING TIP

This shrub is easy to propagate by cutting some healthy new growth in late summer or early autumn (see Semi-ripe cuttings, page 32).

Family Asteraceae	
Height and spread 1–1.5x1–1.5m/3–5x3–5ft	
Habit Bushy	
Flowering time Summer	
Hardiness H4	
Position Full sun	

FOOD FROM OVERSEAS

All brachyglottis – except for one, which occurs in Tasmania – are native to New Zealand. In the UK they are a delight for wildlife and especially for some native butterflies (see also Building a butterfly house, page 48).

Rejuvenating a butterfly bush

It can be very beneficial to cut an entire, very overgrown woody shrub such as butterfly bush (*Buddleja davidii*) down to 10–15cm (4–6in) above ground level, as this encourages it to regrow and develop into a fresh plant, with plenty of new shoots producing flowers throughout summer. Such harsh pruning is also a good way to keep a butterfly bush under control, as otherwise this fast-growing shrub can become very large and unruly. The best time to rejuvenate a butterfly bush is in early spring, when it is coming into growth. Do not be scared of being too brutal – butterfly bush is a very vigorous plant.

1. With secateurs or pruning shears, start by cutting back the top growth so you can see what you are doing better.
2. Then, using loppers, cut back all the thickest branches to open the framework and get better access to the other branches. Prune just above a bud or growing shoot, leaving 10–15cm/4–6in of growth on each branch.
3. Using secateurs, remove the thinnest branches at ground level or leave 10–15cm/4–6in of growth. The aim is to have a strong, well-balanced framework of five or six main branches.
4. Once all the branches have been cut back, fork lightly around the plant to remove any soil compaction. You may want to rake the area to level the soil and remove footprints.

Butterfly bush

Buddleja davidii

Butterfly bush is a Chinese plant that has definitively found its second home in the UK and most other temperate regions of the world. It has a great asset – its familiar, fragrant, purple flowers are adored by butterflies, hence the common name (see also Building a butterfly house, page 48). This large, fast-growing, deciduous shrub has long arching branches and blooms from summer till autumn.

WHERE TO GROW

Plant in autumn in well-drained soil in sun. Butterfly bush grows particularly well in a coastal garden.

HOW TO GROW

Water your plant until well established and then from time to time if there is no rain. Prune back hard in early spring, leaving only a couple of buds on the older branches (see also Rejuvenating a butterfly bush, page 42). Propagate by taking semi-ripe cuttings (see page 32) or hardwood cuttings (see page 34).

GROWING TIP

Deadhead the spent flowers regularly, to encourage more blooms.

A BREEDING CHAMPION
A single flower spike of butterfly bush can produce over 40,000 seeds, which can travel long distances as they are extremely light.

Family
Scrophulariaceae

Height and spread
2.5–4x4–8m/
8–13x13–26ft

Habit Bushy

Flowering time
Summer–autumn

Hardiness H6

Position Sun

OTHER NOTABLE CULTIVARS

- 'Royal Red' is similar in size and shape to the other cultivars but with huge clusters of red-purple flowers.
- 'White Profusion' is less invasive than the species, and produces big clusters of white flowers.

Buddleja davidii 'Royal Red'

Common box

Buxus sempervirens

The common box is an evergreen shrub that has become the shrub for all creative fantasies because it is so often used in topiary. It is indeed of remarkable density with its glossy, dark green leaves. Being slow-growing, really easy to grow and easy to trim, it is ideal for creating a permanent structure in a border or container (see Growing a shrub in a container, page 96). Unfortunately, in recent years the box tree caterpillar (see page 132) and box blight (see page 133) have spread extensively through common box plants.

WHERE TO GROW

This hedging shrub does best in moist but well-drained soil in partial shade. It also tolerates full shade. Ensure that the soil never dries out for too long.

HOW TO GROW

Clip common box twice a year, in early summer and again in early autumn, to maintain the initial shape of the plant. Apply a handful of controlled-release fertilizer around the base of the plant afterwards. Propagate by taking semi-ripe cuttings (see page 32).

GROWING TIP

When applying fertilizer, make sure that it never touches the leaves of the plant.

Family	Buxaceae
Height and spread	4–8x4–8m/ 13–26x13–26ft
Habit	Bushy
Flowering time	Spring
Hardiness	H6
Position	Partial shade

HARD WOOD
Box wood has a very fine grain, which makes it the hardest wood that can be found in the northern hemisphere.

Beauty berry

Callicarpa bodinieri var. *giraldii* aka *C. giraldiana, C. giraldii*

This medium-sized, deciduous shrub gets covered with the most attractive, purple berries in autumn, and they often last until winter. In autumn, too, the dark green leaves turn pink to mauve, and include oranges and reds hues in between.

—

WHERE TO GROW
Plant beauty bush in the middle of a border not too far from the house, where you can enjoy its little berries. Fertile, well-drained soil in sun or partial shade is ideal.

HOW TO GROW
After planting, backfill with a mix of one part garden compost to two parts soil. Water the shrub frequently until well established. In summer, prune the new shoots just above the forming berries. This will tidy up the plant and show off the berries. Propagate by seed or by taking softwood cuttings (see page 31).

GROWING TIP
Plant beauty bush in groups of two or three, to enhance pollination and therefore berry production.

Family Lamiaceae	
Height and spread 2.5–4x1.5–2.5m/ 8–13x5–8ft	
Habit Bushy, upright	
Flowering time Summer	
Hardiness H6	
Position Sun–partial shade	

NOTABLE CULTIVARS

- 'Profusion' produces masses of bright purple berries.
- 'Snowstar' is grown for its shiny, pearl-like, white berries.

A GREEK NAME
Although native of southern China and Indochina, this plant's name – *Callicarpa* – is Greek and means 'beautiful fruit'.

Callicarpa bodinieri var. *giraldii* 'Profusion'

Japanese camellia

Camellia japonica

Japanese camellia is a slow-growing evergreen shrub that is appreciated for its dark green, glossy foliage and impressive display of flowers in winter and spring. Thousands of cultivars are available in a variety of flower sizes, shapes and colours.

WHERE TO GROW

Grow in well-drained, humus-rich, slightly acidic soil that stays moist but not soggy, in a shaded spot sheltered from strong winds. Japanese camellia is an excellent shrub for a container (see Growing a shrub in a container, page 96).

HOW TO GROW

Plant in autumn to encourage the roots to establish. Water well in dry weather. Apply an ericaceous fertilizer in spring and again in early summer. No pruning is needed. Propagate by taking semi-ripe cuttings (see page 32).

GROWING TIP

Japanese camellia does not like hard pruning. If necessary, lightly trim any unwanted branches after flowering.

Family Theaceae

Height and spread
1.5–4x1.5–2.5m/
5–13x5–8ft

Habit Bushy

Flowering time
Winter–spring

Hardiness H5

Position Partial shade–full shade

ANOTHER NOTABLE SPECIES

- *C. sasanqua* has smaller leaves and blooms than *C. japonica* and flowers in autumn and winter.

TEATIME!
A species that we prize every day for its leaves is *C. sinensis*. This is where tea comes from. It is hardy in most places throughout temperate Europe and thrives in a mild and humid climate. To make your very own tea, pick the young leaves in spring and leave them to dry.

Building a butterfly house

Most species of butterflies spend the winter hidden in vegetation or in the ground. Most are not yet butterflies but instead are eggs, caterpillars or chrysalises. In some species, however, it is the adults that hibernate and look for protected hiding places. The little wooden house shown here will offer them shelter from autumn until spring, and help them to survive the cold winter months. They can also retreat into the house at any other time during the year, to hide from predators. In spring, butterflies may use the house while they transform from chrysalises into butterflies. Make sure that you insert a piece of dead wood before closing the house, so that the butterflies can land and rest on it.

It is better to use non-treated wood if you can, so it is free from chemicals.

You will need
- 4 pieces, 30cm/12in long by 15cm/6in wide, of sawn timber, 2cm/¾in thick (for sides)
- 1 piece, 15cm/6in long by 13cm/5in wide, of sawn timber, 2cm/¾in thick (for base)
- 1 piece, 21cm/8½in long by 16cm/6½in wide, of sawn timber, 2cm/¾in thick (for roof)
- 1 post, 1.2m/4ft long, of sawn timber, 7cm/3in by 5cm/2in (for post)
- Pencil or pen
- Saw
- Drill and 8mm-diameter bit
- Jigsaw
- Glasspaper
- Wood screws and screwdriver
- Nails and hammer
- Piece of dead wood
- Black waterproof paint and paintbrush

1. With a pencil, number each of the four side pieces of timber. Then number the base '5', the roof '6' and the post '7'. Optional: cut one end of pieces '3' and '4' at an angle to form the slope of the roof.
2. On piece 2, mark three entry slots, each 15cm/6in long. Drill the ends of each entry slot with a 8mm-diameter bit.
3. Cut each slot from one end to the other, with the jigsaw. Smooth the entrances with glasspaper.
4. Screw together pieces 1, 3 and 4. Fix on the base (piece 5) with screws or nails. Then secure the post (piece 7) with nails, so the box stands upright.
5. Fix the front (piece 2) with screws or nails. Then stand a piece of dead wood inside the box.
6. Secure the roof (piece 6) in place. Paint the lower part of the post with black waterproof paint, up to the point in which it will be in the ground. Choose a dry place in your border, protected from wind and rain, and dig a hole to install the butterfly house in the ground.

Californian lilac 'Puget Blue'

Ceanothus 'Puget Blue'

'Puget Blue' is a bushy evergreen shrub with a very dense, compact habit. It bears small, dark green leaves, which are covered with clusters of lavender-blue flowers in spring and summer. These abundant blooms are a magnet for birds and butterflies (see also Building a butterfly house, page 48).

Family	Rhamnaceae
Height and spread	1.5–2.5x1.5–2.5m/ 5–8x5–8ft
Habit	Bushy
Flowering time	Spring–summer
Hardiness	H4
Position	Sun

WHERE TO GROW

Plant in fertile, well-drained soil in a sunny position protected from cold and drying winds, where there is enough space for 'Puget Blue' to develop – against a sunny wall is ideal. It is also an excellent plant for a hedge or screen (see Planting a hedge, page 126).

HOW TO GROW

Once well established, 'Puget Blue' is drought tolerant. Lightly prune immediately after flowering. Propagate from semi-ripe cuttings in mid- or late summer (see page 32).

GROWING TIP

Although 'Puget Blue' likes full sun, it will appreciate some afternoon shade in hot summer areas.

OTHER NOTABLE CULTIVARS

- *C.* 'Concha' is slightly taller than 'Puget Blue' and bears its deep blue flowers only in late spring.
- *C.* 'Skylark' is smaller than 'Puget Blue' and has clusters of deep blue flowers in early summer.

BLUE CARPET
For beautiful, deep blue ground cover, opt for *C. thyrsiflorus* var. *repens*, which in spring and early summer is covered with light blue flowers. It grows to only 1m/3ft tall.

Japanese quince 'Pink Lady'

Chaenomeles × superba 'Pink Lady'

'Pink Lady' – a cross between *C. japonica* and *C. speciosa* – is a fast-growing, deciduous shrub. In spring, masses of dark pink flowers appear before the leaves. They are followed in autumn by small, yellow, fragrant fruit, which remain on the shrub once the leaves have fallen.

—

WHERE TO GROW

Grow in any fairly moist but well-drained soil. Train your plant against a fence or a wall, or use it as ground cover at the front of the border. Japanese quince is also perfect in a low flowering hedge.

HOW TO GROW

When planting, backfill with a mix of two parts soil and one part well-rotted compost. Space plants 80cm/32in apart if you want to grow them in a hedge (see Planting a hedge, page 126). After flowering, prune back unruly side shoots to five or six leaves, and remove any crossed stems to maintain a nice shape. Otherwise, prune the shrub only when it has reached the height you want. Propagate by taking semi-ripe cuttings (see page 32).

GROWING TIP

Early spring frosts can be a threat for the flowers. To avoid frost damage, protect the blooms with horticultural fleece in the evening. Remove the protection during daytime.

Chaenomeles x superba 'Salmon Horizon'

Family	Rosaceae
Height and spread	1–1.5x1–1.5m/3–5x3–5ft
Habit	Bushy
Flowering time	Spring
Hardiness	H6
Position	Sun–partial shade

OTHER NOTABLE SPECIES AND CULTIVARS

- *C. japonica* 'Sargentii' has thorny stems and, in spring, a profusion of orange-red flowers followed by edible fruit.
- *C. speciosa* 'Geisha Girl' is covered with double, apricot-pink flowers in spring; the aromatic, greenish yellow fruit are edible when cooked.

FOOD FOR ALL

The fruit are a feast for birds. They are also edible for humans when cooked, and make delicious preserves, jams and jellies.

Mexican orange blossom

Choisya ternata

This native of Mexico develops into a compact evergreen shrub and is very popular across Europe. Its fragrant, dark green leaves exude a citrus smell when trimmed. The pure white, highly scented flowers appear in spring and sometimes again in autumn.

—

WHERE TO GROW

Plant in full sun, sheltered from cold winds in fertile, moist but well-drained soil. Mexican orange blossom is a very good, fast-growing shrub for a fragrant evergreen hedge or for creating a lush exotic look in a border (see Planting a hedge, page 126). It also works well in a front garden as it tolerates urban pollution.

HOW TO GROW

Choisya requires a trim only once a year, in spring immediately after flowering, to keep it in shape. Pruning in spring will also encourage a second blooming, in autumn. Propagate by taking semi-ripe cuttings (see page 32).

GROWING TIP

To get more Mexican orange blossom plants, take semi-ripe cuttings between late summer and mid-autumn (see page 32).

Family Rutaceae	
Height and spread 1.5–2.5x1.5–2.5m/ 5–8x5–8ft	
Habit Bushy	
Flowering time Spring, then autumn–winter	
Hardiness H4	
Position Sun	

NOTABLE CULTIVAR AND HYBRID

- Sundance ('Lich') has bright yellow evergreen foliage and white flowers, in spring. Plant in partial shade for better leaf colour.
- *C. × dewitteana* 'Aztec Pearl' is more compact, with narrow, light green leaves and delicately scented, pink-tinged, white flowers.

WHERE IS THE ORANGE?
The common name orange blossom comes from the fact that the flowers look similar to those on an orange tree. However, they don't have an orange smell but rather a lemony scent.

Cretan rock rose

Cistus creticus

The lifespan of this small, short-lived, evergreen, Mediterranean shrub is usually around ten years in ideal growing conditions. Its papery pink flowers with golden yellow stamens appear in summer. They live only one day, but are constantly renewed among the slightly aromatic, almond-green foliage.

—

WHERE TO GROW

Plant in poor sandy soils, perfectly drained, among rocks, in full sun and protected from cold winds. Cretan rock rose is good in a dry garden or coastal area as it is perfectly resistant to drought and salty winds. Once established, it does not like to be moved.

HOW TO GROW

An established Cretan rock rose will not need watering. A light trim after flowering encourages new shoots; avoid hard pruning. Take softwood cuttings in summer (see page 31).

GROWING TIP

Avoid the combination of heat and humidity, by for example watering in hot weather, as it will trigger the development of a fungus that attacks Cretan rock rose and kills it.

Family Cistaceae	
Height and spread 1–1.5x1–1.5m/3–5x3–5ft	
Habit Bushy	
Flowering time Summer	
Hardiness H4	
Position Sun	

FIRE PLEASE
In its natural habitat along the Mediterranean, Cretan rock rose follows the cycle of wildfires. Every ten years or so, fires clear the landscape. Cretan rock rose seeds spread thanks to the heat of the flames and then germinate with the first autumn rains, filling the landscape with a carpet of new plants.

OTHER NOTABLE SPECIES

- *C. albidus* develops pale grey-green, velvety leaves and large pink flowers, in spring, at the ends of the branches.
- *C. ladanifer* has narrow, dark green leaves covered in spring with masses of large, solitary, papery white flowers dotted with burgundy-red spots on the petal bases.
- *C. laurifolius* has strong erect branches, reddish bark and sticky, laurel-like, dark green leaves; white flowers with yellow centres appear in summer.
- *C. populifolius* is a large shrub with sticky branches and poplar-like, fresh green, wavy-margined, aromatic leaves; white flowers develop from burgundy-red buds in summer.

Looking-glass plant 'Pacific Dawn'

Coprosma repens 'Pacific Dawn'

The small, glossy, rounded leaves change colours through the seasons on this compact evergreen shrub. A mix of green, yellow and pink in spring and summer transforms into hues of chocolate-brown, purple and red in winter. Almost invisible flowers appear at the end of summer.

—

WHERE TO GROW

Coprosma needs slightly acidic, moderately fertile, moist but well-drained soil . Grow in a sunny sheltered position outdoors, or under glass in colder climates.

HOW TO GROW

Plant in early spring, digging a hole twice the size of the root ball and backfilling with an equal mix of soil and ericaceous compost. Water regularly until well established. In spring, lightly prune any branches that disturb the symmetry of the plant. Propagate by taking semi-ripe cuttings (see page 32).

GROWING TIP

Protect looking-glass plant during the colder months by applying a 10–15cm/4–6in layer of woody mulch around the base of the plant to shield its roots from the cold and by wrapping it in horticultural fleece before the first frosts.

Family	Rubiaceae
Height and spread	1–1.5x1–1.5m/3–5x3–5ft
Habit	Bushy
Flowering time	Late summer
Hardiness	H3
Position	Sun

ANOTHER NOTABLE CULTIVAR

- *C.* 'Lemon and Lime' is grown for its yellow and lime-green, shiny foliage, turning almost orange in winter.

SUNSET COLOURS
The leaves of *C. repens* 'Tequila Sunrise' are variegated with green and yellow tones in their centres and salmon-pink edges. When the weather gets cold, the pink hues ripen into a dark rich red.

Dogwood 'Midwinter Fire'

Cornus sanguinea 'Midwinter Fire'

There can be no better name for this cultivar, which is treasured for its flamboyant clumps of orange and red stems in winter. At the end of spring, little white flowers appear. They are followed by small round berries, first green then red, becoming dark purple in summer. The green deciduous foliage turns orange and yellow in autumn.

—

WHERE TO GROW

'Midwinter Fire' thrives in any moderately fertile, well-drained soil in full sun or partial shade. However, the best stem colours will develop in full sun. This dogwood looks spectacular when planted en masse or as an informal hedge (see Planting a hedge, page 126).

HOW TO GROW

Water well during the first two or three years after planting, especially if the weather is dry and hot. Wait for a year or two before pruning. Then, every other year, cut all the stems back to ground level just before the buds start to swell in early spring, because the best winter colours appear on new growth. Propagate by taking hardwood cuttings (see page 34).

GROWING TIP

To enjoy the creamy white flowers and the loved-by-birds berries, leave your shrub unpruned since the berries form only on old stems.

Cornus sanguinea

Family Cornaceae
Height and spread 1.5–2x1.5–2m/ 5–7x5–7ft
Habit Suckering
Flowering time Summer
Hardiness H6
Position Sun–partial shade

OTHER NOTABLE SPECIES AND CULTIVARS

- *C. alba* 'Sibirica' develops bright coral-red stems in winter, white flowers in summer and red leaves and bluish white berries in autumn.
- *C. sericea* 'Flaviramea', to 1m/3ft tall, has olive-green stems, which are brightest in winter; the dark green leaves turn red or orange in winter.

LET'S RECYCLE THE STEMS

Being strong and flexible, dogwood stems are good material from which to make eye-catching, low fences (see Creating a decorative edge with dogwood stems, page 56). They can even be used as skewers to roast marshmallows over the fire.

Creating a decorative edge with dogwood stems

At the beginning of spring, it is time to prune dogwoods (*Cornus*). These beautiful shrubs are grown for their colourful stems, which vary from lime-green to bright red, with orange tones. Being flexible and thin, the prunings are ideal for creating small natural decorations in the garden, as are those of hazel (*Corylus*), see page 58. Here I suggest you define a low border by planting the stems in loops that follow one after the other. Such a small, purely decorative barrier is a fun way to reuse dogwood stems.

1 Look for a bushy shrub with long straight stems about 1m/3ft or more long.

2 Cut about 20 stems, or more, depending of the length of the border you want to define.

3 Remove all the leaves and side branches.

4 Make sure you retain as much length as possible. You will end with some irregular or not perfectly straight stems. It doesn't matter, keep all the material you have cut.

5 Push the first stem into the ground where you want to start your border edge. Insert the other end further on, to form a loop. Push the second stem in the middle of loop one and its other end further on, to form a second, overlapping loop. Push the third stem next to the end of the first stem, and form a third loop.

6 Continue to insert stems as many times as you want, depending on the length you want to achieve.

7 Secure all the intersections with garden string.

Cobnut

Corylus avellana

This large deciduous shrub carries both male and female flowers. The golden yellow male catkins appear in late winter and early spring, hanging under bare branches. They are followed by tiny, red, bud-like female flowers. Once pollinated by wind, these will produce the nuts loved by people and squirrels.

—

WHERE TO GROW
Grow in any well-drained soil in sun, although cobnut appreciates a bit of shade in summer. It is perfect for a hedge or hedgerow (see Planting a hedge, page 126).

HOW TO GROW
Between late autumn and early spring, order a bare-root specimen and plant it immediately on receipt into a mix of two parts soil and one part garden compost. Water well until established. For good fruiting, grow at least two different cultivars together. Propagate by simple layering (see page 35) or by removing suckers.

GROWING TIP
Every five years, in late winter or early spring, cut back four of the oldest branches. Such prunings can be twisted, knotted or used as sticks, plant supports or fishing rods.

Family Betulaceae
Height and spread 4–8x4–8m/13–26x 13–26ft
Habit Bushy
Flowering time Spring
Hardiness H6
Position Sun–partial shade

NOTABLE CULTIVAR

- 'Contorta' is a curious shrub with highly distorted, intertwined branches that are particularly visible in winter before the leaves appear.

READY TO PICK
The best way to know if the cobnuts are ready for harvesting is by observing the squirrels. Once they have started snacking on them, rush to your tree to gather them up. If you wait for too long, you won't have any nuts for yourself.

Smoke bush 'Royal Purple'

Cotinus coggygria 'Royal Purple'

Intense, almost translucent purple leaves, finely edged with pink in spring and summer, are one of the highlights of this large deciduous shrub. From mid- to late summer, large, cloudy, pink flowers also cover the shrub. Then in autumn the leaves turn bright red before falling.

—

WHERE TO GROW
'Royal Purple' needs space and rather poor, well-drained, alkaline soil in full sun or partial shade. However, its foliage will be more flamboyant in full sun. It can be planted in a mixed hedge (see Planting a hedge, page 126), at the back of a border, or as a specimen plant in the middle of the lawn.

HOW TO GROW
Once established, this smoke tree is very well adapted to drought and summer heat. Apply a 10–15cm/4–6in layer of organic farmyard manure after pruning. Propagate by semi-ripe cuttings (see page 32).

GROWING TIP
For best flowering, do not prune. However, for bigger leaves and better foliage colours, hard prune in early spring.

Family Anacardiaceae

Height and spread
4–8x4–8m/13–26x 13–26ft

Habit Bushy

Flowering time Summer

Hardiness H5

Position Sun–partial shade

NOTABLE CULTIVARS

- Golden Spirit ('Ancot') has almost rounded, golden yellow leaves that turn warm orange and red; the flowers are fluffy, like clouds of smoke, from mid- to late summer.
- *C.* 'Ruby Glow', to 1.8m/6ft tall and wide, bears masses of pink flowers in summer, and bronze leaves turning yellow, purple and red in autumn.

SMOKE EFFECT
When 'Royal Purple' is in full bloom, it looks as if smoke is coming out of the surrounding vegetation. This characteristic is unique to its genus and is truly beautiful.

Cotinus coggygria

Cotoneaster

Cotoneaster horizontalis

Cotoneaster comes in all shapes and sizes, but *C. horizontalis* is a spreading deciduous shrub. Its flat branches form a distinctive, herringbone pattern and are covered with small, glossy, dark green leaves that turn bright red in autumn. Pink-tinged, white flowers in spring are followed by bright red, little berries in early autumn – a feast for the birds.

WHERE TO GROW

Keep within the boundaries of your garden in any moderately fertile, well-drained soil and even better grow it in a container on a terrace or a patio, in full sun (see Growing a shrub in a container, page 96). This cotoneaster is drought tolerant once established, which means that a dry slope could also be the perfect spot for it.

HOW TO GROW

Plant in spring or autumn and water well until it is established. Light pruning in late spring will maintain its good shape. Propagate by seed or by semi-ripe cuttings (see page 32).

GROWING TIP

When planted on a bank or a slope, cotoneaster is great at reducing erosion.

Family Rosaceae	
Height and spread 0.5–1x1–1.5m/ 1½–3x3–5ft	
Habit Spreading	
Flowering time Spring	
Hardiness H7	
Position Sun	

OTHER NOTABLE SPECIES

- *C. dammeri* is vigorous and makes evergreen ground cover; small, shiny, deep green leaves and tiny white flowers in early summer are followed by bright red berries in autumn.
- *C. franchetii* is a semi-evergreen shrub, to 4m/13ft tall and wide, with clusters of pink and white flowers in early summer followed by bright orange berries in autumn and winter.

BE WARNED
This native of China is listed as an invasive, non-native species in the UK. In countries where *C. horizontalis* is listed as invasive but is still available for sale, its use is restricted to private gardens; it must not be planted in the wild.

Winter daphne

Daphne odora

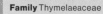

Family Thymelaeaceae	
Height and spread 1–1.5x1–1.5m/3–5x3–5ft	
Habit Bushy	
Flowering time Winter–spring	
Hardiness H4	
Position Sun–partial shade	

Who can resist the powerful exotic fragrance of winter daphne filling a garden for several metres? The pale pink flowers appear from mid-winter to early spring. Because there is little else in bloom at that time, they are an essential source of pollen for bees. This evergreen shrub has dark green leaves.

WHERE TO GROW

Plant in moist but well-drained, alkaline soil, rich in organic matter. Winter daphne prefers partial shade and a mild and humid climate, but can grow in sun. It dislikes being planted in a pot and may not perform very well.

HOW TO GROW

Winter daphne is a little bit capricious and does not like to be moved or have its roots disturbed. It also takes a little while to establish. Pruning is not recommended as it could kill the plant. Keep it to a minimum and wear gloves while doing so, as the sap is an irritant to the skin. Propagate by taking semi-ripe cuttings (see page 32).

GROWING TIP

Every other year in spring, add a 10–15cm/4–6in layer of humus-rich compost around the base of the plant.

POISON

The entire plant is highly toxic but it is winter daphne berries that are extremely poisonous. If your pet might be tempted to eat them, ensure the plant is out of reach.

Beautiful deutzia

Deutzia pulchra

This is one of the best white deutzias, with its pure white, bell-shaped flowers, slightly tinged with pink and filled with golden yellow stamens. It produces deciduous, dark green leaves on graceful arching stems. In winter, the bare copper-coloured branches look like cinnamon sticks.

—

WHERE TO GROW

Beautiful deutzia thrives in any moderately fertile, well-drained, but not too dry, soil in full sun or partial shade, sheltered from cold winds. It is a good shrub for a green and white border.

HOW TO GROW

To encourage strong healthy shoots and improve flowering, prune immediately after flowering. Shorten by one-third all stems bearing faded flowers; also cut any damaged or dead shoots right back to ground level. Propagate by taking softwood cuttings (see page 31) or hardwood cuttings (see page 34).

GROWING TIP

This deutzia can get a bit unkempt if not pruned regularly. If your shrub has become too dense, remove one in three stems right back to ground level. This encourages new basal shoots.

Family Hydrangeaceae	
Height and spread 1.5–2.5x1.5–2.5m/ 5–8x5–8ft	
Habit Bushy	
Flowering time Spring–summer	
Hardiness H4	
Position Sun–partial shade	

OTHER NOTABLE SPECIES AND HYBRIDS

- *D. gracilis* 'Nikko' bears clusters of white flowers in early summer, and is ideal for a small garden.
- *D. × hybrida* 'Mont Rose' is covered with masses of small, tender, lightly scented, star-shaped, pink flowers that turn white once they are fully open in early summer.
- *D. × hybrida* 'Strawberry Fields' bears fragrant, white-edged, mauve-pink flowers in late spring and early summer.

ASIAN BEAUTY
This eye-catching deutzia is native to the Philippines, where it grows in woodland hedges and scrub.

Paperbush

Edgeworthia chrysantha

Luminous, spherical, yellow flower heads appear on bare stems on this small deciduous shrub from late winter to early spring. Their perfume attracts a lot of insects during the darkest days at this time of the year.

—

WHERE TO GROW

Choosing the right place for your paperbush is vital. It needs sun or partial shade, some shelter from wind and loamy, well-drained soil to help it to survive the winter cold. It dislikes soil with a high content of chalk, clay or sand.

HOW TO GROW

When planting, fill up the planting hole with loam-based compost. Once planted, avoid moving your shrub. Water regularly in summer. Paperbush doesn't need pruning – remove only the dead branches. Propagate by taking semi-ripe cuttings (see page 32).

GROWING TIP

To improve the soil and keep soil moist around paperbush in summer, add a 10–15cm/4–6in layer of pine needles around the base of the trunk.

Family Thymelaeaceae

Height and spread 1–1.5x1–1.5m/3–5x3–5ft

Habit Bushy

Flowering time Winter–spring

Hardiness H4

Position Sun–partial shade

NOTABLE CULTIVARS

- 'Grandiflora' bears bigger, more abundant clusters of bright, lightly fragrant, yellow flower heads from late winter to spring. Even though it is rated H4, it is not as hardy as other edgeworthias and needs shelter from a sunny wall when temperatures fall below −5˚C/23˚F.

- 'Red Dragon' has small, orange-red flower clusters in spherical umbels hanging from the tips of bare branches in late winter and early spring.

LUXURY PAPER

Paperbush bark has a parchment-like texture, and in Japan it is used to produce high-quality, handmade paper such as ornamental wallpaper and calligraphy paper.

Making organic nettle-tea fertilizer

Nettle tea is a completely natural product. It is a fertilizer rich in nitrogen, so it promotes the growth of plants while making them more resistant to diseases, and acts as a natural pesticide against insects such as aphids. It also speeds up decomposition of the compost. Using nettle tea instead of chemical products helps your plants while protecting the planet. It is not a curative treatment against diseases but a preventive one, due to its ability to strengthen the natural defences of a plant.

Filter the nettle-tea fertilizer before using it – the fineness depends on whether you apply it with a watering can or through a spray bottle. To keep the solution for several weeks or even a year, it must be finely filtered through a funnel lined with a piece of clean cloth.

The nettle-tea fertilizer is most effective in spring, when the plants are in full growth. A small disadvantage is that it does not smell very good.

You can also make your own liquid feed from comfrey (*Symphytum*), using the same method as for nettles.

You will need

- Protective gardening gloves
- Garden container
- Plastic bucket – never a metal one
- Tea towel
- Clothes pegs
- Wooden stick (optional)
- Funnel
- Large empty plastic container with an airtight cap or lid
- Piece of clean fabric to line the funnel
- Empty jam jar or jug

1 Wearing gloves, harvest 1kg/2¼lb of nettles and place in a convenient garden container.
2 Then put the nettles in the plastic bucket and fill with 10 litres/17½ pints of water. Cover the bucket with a tea towel secured with pegs.
3 Allow to macerate for 24–48 hours if you want to use the solution as a pesticide. If you want to use it as a fertilizer, leave the nettles in the water for fifteen days, stirring the mixture with a wooden stick every two days. When there are no more bubbles in the bucket, fermentation is complete.
4 Insert the funnel in the mouth of the large empty plastic container.
5 Line the funnel with the piece of fabric.
6 Use a jam jar to slowly pour and filter the mixture through the fabric-lined funnel. It can be a bit unpleasant because of the bad smell.
7 Seal the filled container with an airtight cap or lid.

Oleaster 'Quicksilver'

Elaeagnus 'Quicksilver'

'Quicksilver' is a large deciduous shrub grown for its ornamental foliage. Willow-like, metallic-silver leaves are produced on arching branches, which weep at the ends. In summer, tiny, creamy yellow flowers fill the garden with their sweet heady fragrance. They are followed by small yellow berries in autumn.

WHERE TO GROW

Grow in any well-drained soil in sun. 'Quicksilver' tolerates dry conditions and salt-laden air, which makes it suitable for a warm coastal garden.

HOW TO GROW

Lightly prune in late winter or early spring by removing diseased, damaged or crossing branches. Apply a 10–15cm/ 4–6in layer of organic farmyard manure afterwards. Propagate by taking semi-ripe cuttings (see page 32) or by removing suckers.

GROWING TIP

'Quicksilver' produces suckers. These shoots coming from the roots should be removed as close as possible to their point of origin, by tearing them away rather than cutting them, to reduce the possibility of regrowth.

Family	Elaeagnaceae
Height and spread	2.5–4x2.5–4m/8–13x 8–13ft
Habit	Bushy
Flowering time	Summer
Hardiness	H5
Position	Sun

ANOTHER NOTABLE HYBRID AND CULTIVAR

- *E. × submacrophylla* has metallic dark green leaves that are silvery beneath; small, fragrant, white flowers in autumn are followed by red berries in winter.
- *E. × submacrophylla* 'Limelight' bears bicoloured leaves with lime-green contours and yellow-splashed centres, and fragrant, creamy white flowers in autumn.

ENEMY IN THE USA
Russian olive (*E. angustifolia*), which was bought to the USA in the early 1900s as an ornamental shrub and windbreak, is now classified as an invasive plant in that country, especially in coastal areas.

Escallonia 'Apple Blossom'

Escallonia 'Apple Blossom'

Masses of pink and white, tubular flowers, enclosed in basal red calyces, are borne in terminal racemes in summer and early autumn, and their colour and delicacy are reminiscent of apple blossom – hence the cultivar name. This small evergreen shrub also has small, shiny, dark green leaves.

—

WHERE TO GROW

Grow in any well-drained soil in a warm position, protected from cold winds. 'Apple Blossom' is an excellent hedging plant in a coastal area or dry garden (see Planting a hedge, page 126), and flowering shrub in a mixed border.

HOW TO GROW

Plant in spring, or in autumn in frost-free climates. Once established, 'Apple Blossom' is drought tolerant. If your soil is poor, apply a 10–15cm/4–6in layer of organic farmyard manure around the base of the plant in spring. To maintain a nice shape, lightly prune in mid- or late spring by removing any branches that disturb the symmetry of the plant. Propagate by taking softwood cuttings (see page 31), semi-ripe cuttings (see page 32) or hardwood cuttings (see page 34).

GROWING TIP

Deadhead regularly to encourage more blooms.

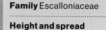

Family Escalloniaceae	
Height and spread 1.5–2.5x1.5–2.5m/ 5–8x5–8ft	
Habit Bushy	
Flowering time Summer	
Hardiness H4	
Position Sun–partial shade	

ANOTHER NOTABLE CULTIVAR

- *E.* 'Iveyi' bears clusters of scented, pure white flowers in mid- and late summer.

HYBRID
'Apple Blossom' is a cross between *E. virgata* and *E. rubra* var. *macrantha*, two species native to South America, particularly Chile and Argentina.

Spindle 'Red Cascade'

Euonymus europaeus 'Red Cascade'

Deciduous 'Red Cascade' is a large open shrub grown for its spectacular autumn colours and ornamental berries. Its dark green leaves turn bright red, making the plant glow with warm hues while the days get darker. Tiny summer flowers are followed by masses of bright pink berries, which open to reveal orange seeds.

—

WHERE TO GROW

Plant in any moist, but well-drained soil in full sun for the best autumn colours. 'Red Cascade' can be used as a specimen plant or screen or in a hedgerow (see Planting a hedge, page 126). It looks good against an evergreen background.

HOW TO GROW

Lightly prune in late winter or early spring to remove any dead, damaged or crossing branches. Apply a 10–15cm/4–6in layer of organic farmyard manure afterwards. Hard pruning is not recommended.

GROWING TIP

Between late summer and mid-autumn, take semi-ripe cuttings from the current season's growth (see page 32). This is an easy way to get more plants at minimal cost.

Family	Celastraceae
Height and spread	2.5–4x1.5–2.5m/ 8–13x5–8ft
Habit	Bushy
Flowering time	Summer
Hardiness	H6
Position	Sun

NOTABLE SPECIES

- *E. alatus* (winged spindle) has curious cork fins running along its branches, hence its common name. In autumn, the leaves turn vibrant shades of red and bright purple, bringing a spectacular display of warm colours. This plant is considered as invasive in some parts of the USA and therefore is not grown in gardens in some parts of that country.

CHARCOAL FOR ARTISTS

The common name spindle comes from the fact that, in the past, the wood was used to make spindles for spinning and holding wool. Today, spindle wood is used to make high-quality charcoal for artists.

Evergreen bittersweet 'Emerald Gaiety'

Euonymus fortunei 'Emerald Gaiety'

This bushy shrub has luminous and attractive foliage comprising small, emerald-green leaves circled with white margins. The leaves can take on a pink tinge in winter. 'Emerald Gaiety' rarely flowers.

—

WHERE TO GROW
Grow in any moist but well-drained soil in full sun or partial shade. 'Emerald Gaiety' should be positioned in the front of a border or around a tree. It also climbs if planted against a wall or a fence.

HOW TO GROW
This easy-to-grow plant requires very little care. Trim stem tips in the first spring after planting, to encourage bushy growth. Remove any plain, green-leaved shoots as soon as they appear.

GROWING TIP
From late summer until mid-autumn, take semi-ripe cuttings to propagate your plant (see page 32).

Family Celastraceae

Height and spread
0.5–1x1–1.5m/
1½–3x3–5ft

Habit Bushy

Flowering time Summer

Hardiness H5

Position Sun–partial shade

NOTABLE CULTIVARS

- 'Emerald 'n' Gold' makes excellent ground cover, with small, bright yellow and dark green leaves, which are often flushed pink in winter.
- 'Silver Queen' produces dark green leaves adorned with creamy white margins that get a pink tint when mature.

SOURCE OF GOOD FORTUNE
The species was introduced into the UK in 1860 by the famous Scottish botanist and plant hunter Robert Fortune, who collected the plant in China along with many others. It is to this remarkable man that we owe the great variety of plants growing in our gardens today.

Spindle 'Bravo'

Euonymus japonicus 'Bravo'

'Bravo' is an evergreen shrub of upright habit. It is extremely versatile and can be grown as a free-standing specimen, as a hedge or be clipped in a topiary. Its glossy oval leaves are green with irregular, creamy white margins. Flowers and berries are tiny and quite insignificant.

—

WHERE TO GROW

Being resistant to sea air, and also to wind, sun and pollution, 'Bravo' is one of those excellent shrubs for a coastal garden. It is happy almost everywhere in sun or partial shade, in a border or in a container on a balcony (see Growing a shrub in a container, page 96). Any well-drained soil is suitable.

HOW TO GROW

This low-maintenance plant does better if planted in spring. (See also Planting a hedge, page 126.) Lightly prune it between mid- and late spring, once there is little risk of frost. Apply a 10–15cm/4–6in layer of organic farmyard manure twice a year, in early spring and autumn. Propagate by semi-ripe cuttings (see page 32).

GROWING TIP

Like many shrubs with variegated leaves, 'Bravo' sometimes reverts to all-yellow or all-green leaves. Therefore, cut out any shoot bearing plain green or plain yellow leaves as soon as it appears.

Family Celastraceae

Height and spread 2.5–4x1.5–2.5m/ 8–13x5–8ft

Habit Bushy

Flowering time Summer

Hardiness H5

Position Sun–partial shade

NOTABLE CULTIVAR

- 'Green Rocket' has lime-green young leaves that mature to dark green.

VICTORIAN FAVOURITE

Because it resisted saline spray and coastal winds, 'Bravo' was the darling of Victorian seaside towns from the early nineteenth century, when it arrived in the UK from Japan.

Pearl bush 'The Bride'

Exochorda × macrantha 'The Bride'

Graceful arching branches give this beautiful deciduous shrub
a weeping appearance. Before its flowers open, the young
branches bear perfectly round, pearly white buds, hence the
name pearl bush. Then in spring it is covered with semi-double,
white flowers. In autumn, the pale green leaves turn yellow and
orange before falling.

WHERE TO GROW
Plant in moist but well-drained, fertile soil in sun or partial
shade. Scorching sun may burn the leaves. To be at its best,
pearl bush needs a suitable space in a good-sized garden.

HOW TO GROW
Add a 10–15cm/4–6in layer of garden compost to the planting
hole. Apply organic farmyard manure once a year in early
spring. Two years after planting and then every other year,
lightly prune after flowering by cutting back the oldest
branches by one-third. Propagate by taking softwood
cuttings (see page 31).

GROWING TIP
Pearl bush flowers on its
previous year's growth.
To give plenty of time for new
growth to develop, always prune
immediately after flowering.

Family Rosaceae

Height and spread
1.5–2.5x1.5–2.5m/
5–8x5–8ft

Habit Arching, bushy

Flowering time
Spring–summer

Hardiness H6

Position Sun–partial
shade

NOT AFRAID
Pearl bush is an extremely
hardy shrub that can resist
temperatures as low as
−20˚C/−4˚F. It makes a splendid
flowering shrub in the regions
of northern Europe where the
winters are very cold.

Creating a jungle garden

If your last holiday in the tropics is a faraway memory, it is possible to bring some exoticism to your garden by planting a selection of plants that will remind you of the lush vegetation in your favourite tropical getaway. Don't be put off if you have a small planting plot. Tropical-looking plants work well in most gardens, and are even better in smaller spaces as they very often make the area seem much larger. Indeed, the dense vegetation with its different types of leaves will give depth to your space.

Evergreen shrubs are ideal for this project, with their glossy leaves of different shapes and sizes. The 'jungle effect' will be achieved by mixing different shades of greens, various types of leaves, and plants of different height and forms. Shrubs alone won't be enough to create the perfect look, so they should be mixed with trees and perennial plants as well. Let's get started!

The first thing to do is to calculate the size of your bed or border. You don't want to end up with too many or not enough plants. Then make a list of plants that could work well together. The all-time favourite shrub for a jungle garden is Japanese aralia (*Fatsia japonica*) for its extra-large, evergreen glossy leaves and easy-to-grow properties. Plant it with Japanese pittosporum (*Pittosporum tobira*) or rakai hebe (*Veronica rakaiensis*). For a sunny border, the great honey flower (*Melianthus major*) looks particularly spectacular. For other plants that go well in a jungle garden, choose between a mix of trees such as Chinese rice-paper plant (*Tetrapanax papyrifer*), palms (for example, Chusan palm/*Trachycarpus fortunei* and cabbage palm/*Cordyline*), tree ferns (*Dicksonia antarctica*), ferns, perennials such as Japanese banana (*Musa basjoo*) and phormiums. Pachysandras make useful ground cover, arum lily (*Zantedeschia*) bears exotic white flowers, and exotic climbers such as passion flower (*Passiflora caerulea*) cover walls and fences well.

Plant your jungle in spring once all risk of frost has passed, in a sheltered spot. Once you have acquired all the plants for your jungle garden, set them on the bed or border, but do not plant them yet. Put any climbers against a wall, the higher trees and shrubs at the back, the medium plants in the middle and the ground-cover ones in the front. Once you are satisfied with the display, plant them and water well. Then wait for the plants to develop into a lush jungle.

A Banana plants, with their huge, paddle-shaped leaves are perfect for that exotic look. They can thrive outside in a warm, sunny, sheltered position with perennials such as cannas, fountain grasses (*Pennisetum advena*) and other colourful ground cover. Banana plants will die back with the first frost, but will come back into leaf the following spring.

B Castor oil plant (*Ricinus communis*), with its large broad leaves and deep purple-red colour, will add a bit of exotic drama to your border. Be aware, though: all parts of this plant are toxic.

C Use the protection of an evergreen hedge such as English yew (*Taxus baccata*) to create your jungle garden. Plants such as tree fern and Japanese banana will appreciate the shelter they need from strong winds and cold winters.

Japanese aralia

Fatsia japonica

This evergreen shrub is very much appreciated for its large, green, exotic-looking leaves, which are 15–30cm/6–12in wide, sometimes more. In winter, this shrub produces clusters of ball-like, white flower heads, which are an essential source of food for insects at this tough time of the year. Decorative black berries often follow the flowers.

—

WHERE TO GROW

Japanese aralia is very often chosen to create an exotic look in the garden (see Creating a jungle garden, page 72). Plant in partial or full shade, sheltered from cold winds. Any moist but well-drained soil is suitable.

HOW TO GROW

Provide moisture in summer and dry soil in winter. Towards the end of spring, remove any unsightly shoots and leaves. If the shrub has become too large, cut the old stems back down to ground level. Propagate by semi-ripe cuttings (see page 32).

GROWING TIP

Planting in spring rather than in autumn is always better for Japanese aralia. Make sure to choose an appropriate spot as Japanese aralia doesn't like to be transplanted.

Family Araliaceae

Height and spread 2.5–4x2.5–4m/8–13x 8–13ft

Habit Bushy

Flowering time Autumn

Hardiness H5

Position Partial shade– full shade

NOTABLE CULTIVAR

- 'Tsumugi-shibori' (aka 'Spider's Web') produces lush, dark green, variegated leaves dusted with a white powder around the edges.

INTER-GENERIC HYBRID

In 1910, in Nantes, France, two nurserymen from the Frères Lizé nursery, created the tree ivy by crossing *Fatsia japonica* 'Moserii' (the seed parent) and Irish ivy (*Hedera helix* 'Hibernica'; the pollen parent). The nurserymen named it × *Fatshedera*, which is derived from the names of the two parent genera. It has only one species, × *Fatshedera lizei*.

Forsythia

Forsythia × intermedia

The arrival of spring is announced by forsythia's profusion of bright golden yellow flowers. They are the sunshine of the garden at this time of year, when not much else is in bloom, and they cover this tough, fast-growing, deciduous shrub, forming a graceful display on the upright, then arching, stems before the dark green leaves appear.

WHERE TO GROW

Plant in any moist, but well-drained soil in full sun or partial shade. Use as a hedge or a screen (see Planting a hedge, page 126), as a background behind the border or as a specimen plant. Forsythia also tolerates coastal salts and winds.

HOW TO GROW

For the first two to three years after planting, let forsythia fully establish and don't prune it. Then, every other year and immediately after flowering, cut back any old, damaged, dead and crossing stems as close to the base as possible. Propagate by taking semi-ripe cuttings (see page 32).

GROWING TIP

Keep an eye out for forsythia gall (see page 135) and carefully prune out any affected branches, which should then be burnt.

Family Oleaceae

Height and spread
2.5x2.5m/8x8ft

Habit Upright, then arching

Flowering time
Early spring

Hardiness H5

Position Sun–partial shade

NOTABLE CULTIVARS

- 'Goldrausch' bears larger and more abundant flowers than the other cultivars; they totally cover the plant in early spring.
- 'Lynwood Variety', to 3m/10ft tall and wide, brightens up the garden from late winter to early spring with its mass of very bright yellow flowers covering its bare branches.

GOOD FOR BOUQUETS

Forsythia stems in bloom or in full leaf are very nice for cutting for flower arrangements (see also Drying hydrangea blooms for flower arrangements, page 82).

Fuchsia 'Genii'

Fuchsia 'Genii'

Among numerous fuchsia cultivars is 'Genii', a small hardy variety that can be grown outdoor in mild areas where frost is not too intense. Small, delicate, red and purple flowers hang on reddish stems from early summer to mid-autumn. They contrast nicely with the lime-green, deciduous foliage.

—

WHERE TO GROW

Grow in a small garden or a container, sheltered from cold drying winds (see Growing a shrub in a container, page 96). Although 'Genii' needs a lot of light to flower, it cannot tolerate scorching sun in summer. A sunny or partially shaded position in fertile, moist but well-drained soil will give your plant the best chance to thrive.

HOW TO GROW

Water regularly as 'Genii' does not like dry soil. If it is planted in a container, feed once a month with liquid fertilizer. Each spring, cut back all shoots to near ground level to encourage the development of fresh growth. Propagate by taking softwood cuttings (see page 31) or semi-ripe cuttings (see page 32).

GROWING TIP

To help 'Genii' survive the cold winter months, apply a 10–15cm/4–6in layer of mulch around its base before the first frosts.

Family Onagraceae	
Height and spread 50–100x10–50cm/ 20–39x4–20in	
Habit Bushy	
Flowering time Early summer–mid-autumn	
Hardiness H4	
Position Sun–partial shade	

A FRENCH DISCOVERY
The French botanist and explorer Charles Plumier, in the late seventeenth century, discovered *Fuchsia* (*triphylla*) on the Caribbean island of Hispaniola (today Haiti and the Dominican Republic).

OTHER NOTABLE CULTIVARS

- *F.* 'Hawkshead' produces small, dark green leaves and masses of single white flowers from midsummer until the first frosts of autumn.
- *F.* 'Riccartonii' is hardier (H6), with small to medium-sized flowers bearing crimson tubes and sepals, and deep purple petals.
- *F.* 'Tom West' Meillez is more tender (H2) and has variegated, cream and almond-green leaves with pink margins and veins, as well as a profusion of small, red and purple, single flowers.

New Zealand broadleaf

Griselinia littoralis

In its country of origin, New Zealand, this upright, evergreen, fast-growing shrub grows in forests along the coast – its rounded, glossy, apple-green foliage being resistant to sea spray and coastal winds. Little, yellow-green flowers appear in spring and are followed by purple berries on the female plant.

—

WHERE TO GROW

New Zealand broadleaf makes an excellent hedging plant (see Planting a hedge, page 126) or a windbreak in mild seaside climates. It can also be grown in a container (see Growing a shrub in a container, page 96). Plant it in light, fertile and well-drained soil protected from severe cold. See also Creating a jungle garden, page 72.

HOW TO GROW

Water well until established but make sure the soil is free-draining and not waterlogged. In spring, lightly cut back any shoots that disturb the symmetry of the plant; otherwise, it needs no other pruning. Propagate by taking semi-ripe cuttings (see page 32).

GROWING TIP

If grown as a hedge, New Zealand broadleaf can be pruned in summer, preferably using hedging shears. Avoid cutting into old wood.

Family	Griseliniaceae
Height and spread	4–8x2.5–4m/13–26x 8–13ft
Habit	Bushy
Flowering time	Spring
Hardiness	H5
Position	Sun

NOTABLE CULTIVAR

- 'Variegata', to 2.5m/8ft tall, has variegated, rounded, apple-green leaves circled with irregular, creamy white margins.

HEALING BARK
Before modern medicine became available, Māori people used the bark of *Griselinia littoralis* to treat skin infections.

Griselinia littoralis 'Variegata'

Witch hazel 'Pallida'

Hamamelis × intermedia 'Pallida'

This elegant deciduous shrub is most appreciated in winter, when its bare branches are covered with ribbon-petalled, yellow flowers. They are sweetly scented and very resistant to frost and snow, and appear before the bright green leaves. In autumn, the foliage turns golden yellow before falling.

—

WHERE TO GROW
'Pallida' makes a very good focal point when planted in a lawn. It also does well in a winter garden with evergreen shrubs such as camellias, daphnes or sweet box (*Sarcococca*). It likes slightly acid, moderately fertile, moist but well-drained soil in sun or partial shade.

HOW TO GROW
In early spring, apply a 10–15cm/4–6in layer of ericaceous compost around the base of the plant to avoid yellowing of the leaves. Immediately after flowering, remove any unwanted or damaged branches. Propagate by grafting.

GROWING TIP
Always apply a 10–15cm/4–6in layer of well-rotted organic farmyard manure after pruning. Choose a rather acid mulch if your soil is on the alkaline side (pH 8).

Family
Hamamelidaceae

Height and spread
2.5–4x2.5–4m/8–13x 8–13ft

Habit Bushy

Flowering time Winter

Hardiness H5

Position Sun–partial shade

NOTABLE CULTIVARS

- 'Diane' has a more open, vase shape and clusters of scented red flowers; in autumn, the foliage reveals different tones of yellow, orange and red.
- 'Jelena' has apricot-orange flowers and beautiful foliage in shades of yellow, orange and red in autumn.
- 'Orange Peel', to 4m/13ft tall, bears deep orange and sweetly scented flowers; in autumn, the leaves develop rich tones of orange, yellow and red before falling.

SKIN BENEFITS
Hamamelis water has been used for centuries as an antioxidant, anti-inflammatory and astringent lotion. It is useful for skin toning, cleaning, calming and healing. Today, renowned skincare companies use hamamelis water in their toners, cleaners and make-up removers.

Curry plant

Helichrysum italicum

For a very intense curry scent, which embalms the air during hot and dry summer days, opt for curry plant. This small evergreen subshrub has aromatic silver leaves similar in shape to that of lavender (*Lavandula*). In summer, the plant produces clusters of small, lemon-yellow flowers.

—

WHERE TO GROW

Grow in full sun in poor, very well-drained soil. Curry plant looks fabulous in a Mediterranean garden or gravel garden, or plant it in a pot where it can perfume your terrace or your balcony. Protect it from winter wet and cold winds.

HOW TO GROW

Easy-to-grow curry plant is drought tolerant and requires little watering. Prune lightly in spring to keep the plant compact. Propagate by semi-ripe cuttings in summer (see page 32).

GROWING TIP

Curry plant flowers are perfect for dry flower arrangements since they retain their colour for a very long time.

Family Asteraceae
Height and spread 10–50x50–100cm/ 4–20x20–39in
Habit Bushy
Flowering time Summer
Hardiness H4
Position Sun

OTHER NOTABLE SPECIES

- *H. petiolare*, H3, is a creeping perennial that forms bright silver domes.
- *H. stoechas* is a semi-evergreen shrub or woody-based perennial with lavender-like, silvery leaves. In summer, the bright yellow flowers cluster together to form a bouquet.

HERBAL MEDICINE

In traditional medicine, the essential oil of curry plant helps to dissolve the bruises of the skin and the blues of the soul. It is also used to heal burns, scars and rashes, as well as emotional wounds.

Smooth hydrangea

Hydrangea arborescens

Recognizable for its slender stems and masses of large, creamy white globes of florets is smooth hydrangea. This medium-sized deciduous shrub also has oval, soft green leaves. The florets and the foliage change colour as they mature, from lime-green to creamy white for the florets, and from soft green to butter-yellow for the leaves.

—

WHERE TO GROW
This species needs sun or partial shade and looks beautiful under the light shade of a tree. If space is not an issue, smooth hydrangea is even better when planted in groups. Grow in humus-rich, moist but well-drained soil.

HOW TO GROW
Water well until well established and even more if planted in full sun – smooth hydrangea does not like to dry out. Prune in early spring to encourage vigorous new growth. For larger flower heads, hard prune to the lowest pair of healthy buds. Deadhead faded flower heads in early to midsummer; thereafter, leave the inflorescence to protect the young buds from frost in winter. For dried floral arrangements, cut the flowered stems in early autumn (see Drying hydrangea for flower arrangements, page 82). Propagate by taking softwood cuttings (see page 31) or hardwood cuttings (see page 34).

GROWING TIP
Smooth hydrangea flower heads are so big that the stems may need some support. Bamboo sticks or ready-made plant supports are ideal.

Family Hydrangeaceae

Height and spread 1–1.5x1.5–2.5m/3–5x5–8ft

Habit Bushy

Flowering time Summer

Hardiness H5

Position Sun–partial shade

NOTABLE CULTIVAR

- 'Annabelle' has enormous, creamy white flower heads that look like giant snowballs, in late summer; young florets are green, they then turn cream and pure white while they mature.

FLOWERS FOR YOUR HOME
Hydrangea flower heads are often used in dried flower arrangements (see Drying hydrangea for flower arrangements, page 82).

Big-leaf hydrangea

Hydrangea macrophylla

The most common of all hydrangeas are deciduous shrubs with large oval leaves. Such big-leaf hydrangeas are divided into two groups: mopheads (with large rounded flower heads) and lacecaps (with much flatter and smaller flower heads, 'flying' like little butterflies around a central cluster of tiny florets).

Family Hydrangeaceae	
Height and spread 1–1.5x1.5–2.5m/ 3–5x5–8ft	
Habit Bushy	
Flowering time Summer	
Hardiness H5	
Position Partial shade	

WHERE TO GROW

Grow in partial shade in moderately fertile, moist but well-drained soil, sheltered from cold drying winds.

HOW TO GROW

Plant in spring or early autumn. Give plenty of water if it is not raining (especially in summer). Every spring, remove the spent flower heads by cutting back the flowered stems to a pair of healthy buds. Prune any dead, old or crossing branches right back to the base. For dried floral arrangements, cut the flowered stems in early autumn (see Drying hydrangea blooms for flower arrangements, page 82). Propagate by taking softwood cuttings (see page 31).

GROWING TIP

To get blue flower heads you need soil of pH 5.2–5.5. To lower the soil pH, apply an acidic mulch such as conifer clippings or pine needles. Be aware, white hydrangea flowers will never turn blue.

NOTABLE CULTIVARS

- 'Ayesha' (mophead) is covered with lilac-like, slightly scented flower heads in early summer.
- 'Mariesii Perfecta' (lacecap) carries flattened, lavender-blue flower heads in summer.
- *H.* Miss Saori (mophead) flowers on both new and old wood; the florets are bicoloured with pinkish red margins and creamy white centres.
- 'Zorro' (lacecap) bears blue flower heads on deep purple-black stems; they turn bright pink in alkaline soils.

Drying hydrangea blooms for flower arrangements

In no time at all, it is very easy to create a wonderful bouquet that will last for many months. This project is with big-leaf hydrangea (*Hydrangea macrophylla*; see page 81) flowers, but other hydrangea species can be used. For example, those of smooth hydrangea (*H. arborescens*) 'Annabelle' (see page 80) mixed with some greens from the garden are also beautiful fresh or dry.

Flowers for drying must be cut only in early autumn – never earlier than this and never later. They should still be in full bloom but going towards the end of flowering so they are no longer full of sap. Often at this time, the little florets change colour, which makes the combination even more beautiful. You can create as many bouquets as you want, of different sizes depending on the number of flowers stems you have tied together.

1 With secateurs, cut as many flower heads as you want (here of big-leaf hydrangea), but choose ones with rigid long stems and harmonious flower-head shapes.
2 With your fingers or secateurs, remove all but the uppermost leaves along the entire length of the stems.
3 Arrange the flower stems together and hold them firmly with one hand.
4 Tie string around the bouquet at the stem tops, so that the flowers stay in place.
5 Depending on the depth of your vase, cut any excess from the stems, with secateurs. The stems should not show once the flowers are place in their vase.
6 Place your bouquet in the vase. Do not put any water in it.

Paniculate hydrangea

Hydrangea paniculata

A paniculate hydrangea is a robust, rather large, deciduous shrub with conical elongated inflorescences called panicles. They are green, pink or white until mid-autumn, when they change colour, gradually turning pink then brown. The dark green leaves also assume some autumn colours, turning into shades of red.

WHERE TO GROW

Unlike big-leaf hydrangea (see page 81), paniculate hydrangea needs sun and light to produce beautiful blooms but does tolerate partial shade. It thrives in humus-rich, moist but well-drained soil. Use as a flowering hedge (see Planting a hedge, page 126) or as a specimen plant at the back of a border.

HOW TO GROW

Give plenty of water until well established. Paniculate hydrangea is more drought tolerant than other hydrangeas. To get bigger blooms, prune in early spring. This species responds well to hard pruning. Propagate by taking softwood cuttings (see page 31).

GROWING TIP

The unique, cone-shaped flower heads, which develop on high upright shoots, are perfect for flower arrangements. Cut them fresh or dry them in early autumn for a beautiful bouquet or a centrepiece (see Drying hydrangea blooms for flower arrangements, page 82).

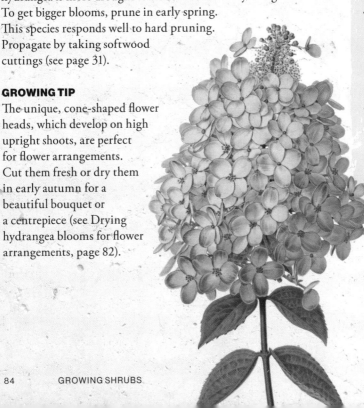

Family Hydrangeaceae

Height and spread 1–2.5x1.5–2.5m/ 3–8x5–8ft

Habit Bushy

Flowering time Summer–mid-autumn

Hardiness H5

Position Sun–partial shade

NOTABLE CULTIVARS

- 'Jane' (aka 'Little Lime') bears large panicles of soft lime-green florets in late summer that turns white and then blush-pink when more mature.
- 'Limelight' carries masses of enormous flower heads, to 30cm/12in long; they mature from a fresh lime-green to a deep pink before fading to beige in autumn.
- 'Wim's Red' develops burgundy-red stems on which, from spring to autumn, are borne clusters of honey-scented, white flowers, which mature to pink and then rich red.

Rose of Sharon

Hypericum calycinum

This spreading evergreen shrub produces dark green to bluish green foliage. Large, saucer-shaped, bright yellow flowers are borne on slender stems for a very long period, from midsummer to mid-autumn. Each flower presents a prominent crown of golden yellow stamens.

—

WHERE TO GROW

Rose of Sharon grows absolutely everywhere except in waterlogged soils. It produces more flowers in full sun, but also thrives in partial shade and even full shade. It is ideal for under a tree or planted en masse as ground cover on a bank or slope.

HOW TO GROW

One of the easiest shrubs to grow, it is also fast-growing and invasive. Regularly remove the stems that develop on the periphery of this shrub to leave space for other plants. If it is planted as a single shrub, prune hard immediately after flowering, with garden shears, to increase flowering. Propagate by taking semi-ripe cuttings (see page 32).

GROWING TIP

Every other year in late winter or early spring, clip or even mow rose of Sharon to promote new growth.

Family Hypericaceae	
Height and spread 0.5–1x1–1.5m/ 1½–3x3–5ft	
Habit Suckering	
Flowering time Summer–autumn	
Hardiness H5	
Position Sun–full shade	

NOTABLE HYBRIDS

- *H. × hidcoteense* 'Hidcote' is evergreen or semi-evergreen, and bushy, with dark green foliage and large, cup-shaped, golden yellow flowers, which last from summer to autumn.
- *H. x moserianum* 'Tricolor' is semi-evergreen, with eye-catching leaves, coloured green, cream and pink, as well as deep yellow, cup-shaped flowers from midsummer to mid-autumn.

A WEED OR NOT A WEED?

Rose of Sharon, native to Turkey and Bulgaria, is almost indestructible and sometimes despised as an invasive weed. This is one of the reasons why hybrids such as *H. × moserianum* or *H. × hidcoteense* exist so you don't need to fear that giant hypericum bed in your garden.

Japanese holly

Ilex crenata aka box-leaved holly

This slow-growing, evergreen shrub is now often chosen as an alternative to box (*Buxus*) because it is not (yet) affected by box blight (see page 133) or box tree moth (see Box tree caterpillar, page 132). It has tiny, glossy, deep green leaves, discreet white flowers in late spring and shiny black berries on female plants in autumn.

—

WHERE TO GROW
Japanese holly makes an attractive low hedge (see Planting a hedge, page 126) or year-round focal point if clipped into a ball or any other shape. It thrives in full sun or partial shade in moist but well-drained, humus-rich, slightly acidic soil.

HOW TO GROW
Trim plants grown as a hedge or topiary, in late summer. Always apply a 10–15cm/4–6in layer of organic farmyard manure afterwards. Propagate by semi-ripe cuttings (see page 32) or hardwood cuttings (see page 34).

GROWING TIP
Once established, Japanese holly can cope with a bit of drought, but not for too long.

Family Aquifoliaceae

Height and spread 4–8x1–1.5m/13–26x 3–5ft

Habit Bushy

Flowering time Summer

Hardiness H6

Position Sun–partial shade

NOTABLE CULTIVARS

- 'Convexa' has very shiny, tiny leaves, which are often clipped as topiary; as it is female it will produce plenty of glossy black berries in autumn if a male holly is growing nearby.
- 'Golden Gem', to 1m/3ft tall, is ideal for a low evergreen hedge with its golden yellow leaves that turn lime-green in autumn. Being female, it needs a male holly tree growing alongside if it is to flower and fruit.

Ilex crenata 'Carolina Upright'

BONSAI FAVOURITE
Japanese holly is frequently grown into a bonsai tree, as enthusiasts appreciate its dense evergreen foliage and tiny glossy leaves.

Double-flowered Japanese rose

Kerria japonica 'Pleniflora'

Masses of pompom-like, bright yellow flowers cover this graceful deciduous flowering shrub from mid- to late spring. They are borne on slender arching stems and resemble small roses. The leaves are prominently veined and light green.

—

WHERE TO GROW

Grow double-flowered Japanese rose as a specimen plant in a shrub border or in a group in an informal hedge (see Planting a hedge, page 126). It likes rich, well-drained soil in sun or partial shade; however, flowers can fade quicker in full sun.

HOW TO GROW

Plant between late autumn and late winter in frost-free soil to enjoy its blooms in spring. Double-flowered Japanese rose flowers on the previous year's growth; therefore, remove the old stems in spring immediately after flowering to maximize the flower show for the following year. Propagate by taking semi-ripe cuttings (see page 32).

GROWING TIP

Remove unwanted suckers regularly to prevent this shrub becoming too invasive (see page 27).

NOTABLE CULTIVAR

- 'Golden Guinea', to 1.5m/5ft tall, bears single, solitary, golden yellow flowers on arching stems, in spring, and bright green, lance-shaped leaves.

Family Rosaceae	
Height and spread 2.5–4x1.5–2.5m/ 8–13x5–8ft	
Habit Suckering	
Flowering time Mid–late spring	
Hardiness H5	
Position Sun–partial shade	

ONE SPECIES ONLY

Kerria japonica is native to China, Japan and Korea. It belongs to the rose family (Rosaceae) and is the only species in its genus.

Dried lavender flower bag

The scent of lavender (*Lavandula*) flowers has the power to immediately transport you to the hills of Haute Provence, in France, illuminated by the July sun and lulled by the songs of cicadas, where lavender thrives. Dried lavender flowers retain their fragrance for a very long time, and the Romans were known to use them not only for their culinary and medicinal properties, but also to perfume their clothes and their baths.

The part of lavender that you need to harvest for this project are the flower buds and the flowers themselves. The best time to do this is on a dry day, at the end of the summer, once your lavender is about to finish flowering. It is also the time to prune your lavender, and using the prunings to make lavender bags is a perfect way to recycle your cuttings. You can place your bag in a cupboard or drawer, where it will perfume your laundry for years.

You will need
- Lavender flowering stems
- Secateurs
- Bowl
- Piece of patterned cotton fabric, 15×15cm/6×6in
- Piece of plain cotton fabric, 15×15cm/6×6in
- Pins
- Sewing machine and cotton thread
- Pair of scissors
- Small stick
- Spoon
- Sewing needle

1 On a dry summer day, cut lavender flowering stems all the way down to some green growth. Avoid cutting into the woody part of the growth. Remove the bare stems, and retain only the flower heads. Leave them to dry in a bowl for about two weeks.
2 Place the fabric pieces right sides together, secure with pins on four sides, 1cm/½in from the edges of the fabric.
3 Using a sewing machine, sew three of the sides.
4 Sew the fourth side, leaving 2cm/¾in without stitching in the middle of the seam.
5 With scissors, remove the excess fabric on the four sides. Turn the fabric bag inside out, through the gap left on side four. Push out the corners with a stick so that they are well formed.
6 Fill up the fabric bag with dried lavender flowers through the gap on side four.
7 Once your bag is nicely full, close the gap opening by hand sewing with thread and a needle.

English lavender

Lavandula angustifolia

In the shrub kingdom, the lavender is queen. It is undoubtedly the most beloved plant, grown for its unique perfume and distinctive flowers. It even has its very own colour – lavender-blue. English lavender is a compact, evergreen shrub. Its narrow, silver-green leaves are scented as well as its deep blue flowers, which can be used to make soap (see Making rosemary and lavender soap, page 112).

Family Lamiaceae	
Height and spread 0.5–1x1–1.5m/ 1½–3x3–5ft	
Habit Bushy	
Flowering time Summer	
Hardiness H5	
Position Sun	

WHERE TO GROW
Needs poor, very free-draining, sandy (even stony) soils in full sun; avoid heavy, wet soil and shade. English lavender can be used in a border, rock garden, container (see Growing a shrub in a container, page 96) or low flowering hedge (see Planting a hedge, page 126).

HOW TO GROW
Newly planted lavender needs regular watering only during its first summer. After that, it is drought tolerant. However, English lavender in a pot always requires a bit of water in dry hot weather. Prune right after flowering by cutting the green part of the stem; don't cut back into the woody part of it. Propagate by taking semi-ripe cuttings (see page 32).

GROWING TIP
When pruning after flowering, keep the spent flowers to make sachets, which can perfume cupboards and drawers with their wonderful scent (see Dried lavender flower bag, page 88).

FAME INDEED
Lavender has been used for more than 2,500 years for fragrances, therapeutics and aromatics. In fact, lavender was an extremely important (and expensive) source of perfume for the ancient Romans, who used it to scent their hair, baths and clothes. It was also chewed by women to mask the smell of alcohol, as wine was forbidden to Roman women.

Tea tree

Leptospermum scoparium

The very fine, needle-like leaves on this delicate evergreen shrub, native to New Zealand, south-eastern Australia and the Chatham Islands, release their scent when crushed. In late spring and early summer, cup-shaped, white flowers appear along the branches. They are followed by tiny woody capsules containing the seeds.

Family Myrtaceae	
Height and spread 1.5–2.5x1.5–2.5m/ 5–8x5–8ft	
Habit Bushy	
Flowering time Spring–summer	
Hardiness H4	
Position Sun	

WHERE TO GROW

Tea tree needs a sheltered position in full sun. Protect young plants from severe cold. The plant does well in poor, dry, sandy soil, which makes it the perfect companion for other Mediterranean plants.

HOW TO GROW

Prune lightly after flowering to maintain a compact shape and to improve flowering. Be careful not to cut into the woody parts of the stems, as new growth will not develop from there. Propagate by taking semi-ripe cuttings (see page 32).

GROWING TIP

If you live in a frost-prone area, plant tea tree in a pot so it can be moved indoors during winter, away from frosts.

HONEY HONEY

The luxurious manuka honey comes from tea-tree flowers, while its aromatic leaves are a source of an essential oil used by the Māori people. This should not be confused with tea-tree oil, which comes from the Australian shrub *Melaleuca alternifolia*.

OTHER NOTABLE CULTIVARS

- 'Red Damask' is covered in a profusion of deep red flowers, looking like little double roses, from spring to summer; these contrast beautifully with its dark green leaves.
- 'Silver Sheen' has silver leaves on red stems. White buds emerge in late winter, and by early summer they open to reveal double white flowers with dark centres.

Leptospermum scoparium 'Red Damask'

Garden privet

Ligustrum ovalifolium

Garden privet is mostly seen in hedge form but we may forget that it is also a beautiful flowering shrub with fragrant, creamy white flowers. These are borne in panicles in summer and are a magnet for bees. They are followed by small black berries in autumn. The foliage is dense, semi-evergreen and composed of small, bright green leaves.

—

WHERE TO GROW

Garden privet is very tolerant of pollution so use it as a hedge in an urban garden. Alternatively, let it develop freely in a shrub border to enjoy its fragrant melliferous flowers, which have pollen and nectar that can be harvested by honey bees.

HOW TO GROW

When planting, leave 30cm/12in between each plant (see also Planting a hedge, page 126). After planting, apply a 10–15cm/4–6in layer of organic farmyard manure and water well. If the weather is dry, keep watering for two years after planting. If grown as a shrub, garden privet requires little pruning. If grown as a hedge, trim it twice a year, once in late spring and again in late summer. Propagate by taking semi-ripe cuttings (see page 32) or hardwood cuttings (see page 34).

GROWING TIP

An economical way to create a new hedge is to buy bare-root privet plants.

Family	Oleaceae
Height and spread	4–8x2.5–4m/13–26x 8–13ft
Habit	Bushy
Flowering time	Summer
Hardiness	H4
Position	Sun

NOTABLE CULTIVAR AND OTHER NOTABLE SPECIES

- 'Aureum' (golden privet) has leaves variegated with yellow margins and soft green centres.
- *L. japonicum* (Japanese privet) 'Rotundifolium' is a slow-growing, compact, evergreen shrub with glossy, dark green leaves.
- *L. vulgare* (common privet) has a bushy habit, which provides a great nesting site for birds, while its white flowers are loved by bees and butterflies.

STAR OF THE HEDGE
Garden privet is possibly the most widely used hedging plant in England. At some point, privet hedges were so popular in Hampstead Garden Suburb that today they are still marking most property boundaries in that part of north London.

Wilson's honeysuckle

Lonicera ligustrina var. *yunnanensis*

This honeysuckle is very different from its famous climbing cousins. Wilson's honeysuckle is a dense evergreen shrub with a bushy, even spreading habit. Its tiny, *Buxus*-like leaves are borne on long arching stems. Little, creamy white flowers appear in spring but are almost insignificant.

—

WHERE TO GROW

This plant tolerates all soils, but prefers a fertile, moist but well-drained one. It is an excellent shrub for a low or medium-height hedge (see Planting a hedge, page 126). It can also be clipped into topiary.

HOW TO GROW

If grown as a hedge or topiary, clip Wilson's honeysuckle regularly from spring to autumn, to maintain the desired shape. Propagate by taking semi-ripe cuttings (see page 32).

GROWING TIP

Wilson's honeysuckle is a good substitute for common box (*Buxus sempervirens*; see page 45) as it can be clipped into any shape and is resistant to the diseases that affect the box, such as box blight (see page 133) and the box tree caterpillar (see page 132).

Family Caprifoliaceae	
Height and spread 2.5–4x2.5–4m/8–13x 8–13ft	
Habit Bushy	
Flowering time Spring	
Hardiness H6	
Position Sun–partial shade	

ALTITUDE
The species *Lonicera ligustrina* is native to China, from the Yunnan and West Sichuan provinces, where it grows in scrub alongside streams at 1,200–3,000m/ 4,000–10,000ft.

NOTABLE CULTIVARS

- 'Lemon Beauty' bears variegated, dark green leaves with yellow-white margins; the best leaf colours are produced in full sun.

- 'Maigrün' (aka 'Maygreen'), to 1.5m/5ft tall and wide, has very small, glossy, bright green leaves and does very well in shade under a tree where little else will grow.

Loropetalum

Loropetalum chinense

The long arching branches of this dense, spreading, evergreen shrub carry lightly scented, white flowers, comprising four long, ribbon-like petals akin to those of witch hazel (*Hamamelis*; see page 78), from late winter until late spring. Many varieties have deep purple or burgundy leaves.

—

WHERE TO GROW

Plant this species in fertile, well-drained soil, preferably acidic (pH 4.5–6.5), in a sheltered position in sun or partial shade. In areas where temperatures dip below −5°C/23°F, grow it in a pot so it can be moved indoors for winter protection.

HOW TO GROW

Water well once or twice a week until the shrub is well established. Keep pruning to a minimum, and if needed always do so after flowering. Propagate by semi-ripe cuttings (see page 32).

GROWING TIP

Regularly water loropetalum growing in a pot so that the soil never dries out for too long. Make sure there is sufficient drainage in the pot to avoid the soil getting waterlogged and raise the pot slightly to allow the water to escape freely.

Family	Hamamelidaceae
Height and spread	2.5–4x2.5–4m/8–13x 8–13ft
Habit	Bushy
Flowering time	Late winter–late spring
Hardiness	H3
Position	Sun–partial shade

NOTABLE CULTIVAR

- var. *rubrum* 'Fire Dance' has spectacular, lightly scented, raspberry-pink flowers, which look like little spiders and offer a beautiful contrast against the dark purple foliage.

EASTERN PROMISE

Loropetalum is a very good source of nectar for bees at the start of the growing season in the woodlands of China, Japan and the Himalayas, where it is native.

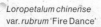

Loropetalum chinense var. *rubrum* 'Fire Dance'

Star magnolia

Magnolia stellata

Star magnolia is grown as a large shrub or small tree, and is the one of the earliest of the spring-flowering magnolias. Pure white, scented, star-shaped flowers appear before the leaves in early spring. They are followed by dark green, oval leaves, which turn golden yellow in autumn before falling.

—

WHERE TO GROW

Grow in a large container (see Growing a shrub in a container, page 96) or in the garden as a specimen plant in any moist but well-drained, acid to neutral soil. Choose a sheltered position to protect the plant and its flowers from strong winds and late frosts.

HOW TO GROW

Every spring, apply a 10–15cm/4–6in layer of organic farmyard manure or leafmould at the base of the shrub. Otherwise, this slow-growing but easy-to-grow shrub requires little maintenance. Keep pruning to a minimum by removing any broken, diseased or crossing branches in midsummer. Propagate by taking softwood cuttings (see page 31) or semi-ripe cuttings (see page 32).

GROWING TIP

Avoid planting anything under the shrub's canopy as it does not like competition with other plants.

Family Magnoliaceae	
Height and spread 1.5–2.5x2.5–4m/ 5–8x8–13ft	
Habit Bushy	
Flowering time Early spring	
Hardiness H6	
Position Sun–partial shade	

OTHER NOTABLE HYBRID AND CULTIVAR

- *M. × soulangeana* bears large, very fragrant, tulip-shaped, white flowers flushed with pink, in late spring, followed by dark green, glossy foliage.
- *M.* 'Susan' has vibrant purple-pink flowers emerging from red-purple buds from mid-spring to midsummer.

VERY OLD
The oldest fossils of magnolias date back to some 90 million years ago, which means that magnolias are among the most primitive flowering plants.

Growing a shrub in a container

Many shrubs are happy in containers, but there are a few things that need to be done to help them to thrive. One of the most important decisions is to choose an appropriately sized container in which to plant your shrub – bigger is better when it comes to pot size. Bigger pots tend to retain moisture for longer and give shrubs enough space to develop their root systems. Larger pots are also heavier and therefore more suitable to support the weight of the plants. Good drainage is also essential, so make sure that the container has at least one drainage hole. This way, the risk of waterlogged soil is reduced. In cold climates, a frost-proof pot is highly recommended.

Because shrubs in containers have limited access to nutrients, it is important to grow them in soil that is suitable for containers, such as good-quality multipurpose potting compost. (Check the information on the packaging before buying.) Such soils contain all the nutrients your plants need for a good start. They also provide good aeration and good drainage. Acid-loving plants such as azaleas and camellias require ericaceous potting compost.

When ready to start planting your shrub, position the container on feet or bricks, to facilitate water drainage, and place some crocks of broken pottery or tiles or some stones in the base of the pot. This will prevent the drainage hole getting obstructed with soil. Then add a layer of grit before half-filling the pot with potting compost.

Place the shrub in the centre and adjust its depth until the top of the root ball is just (2cm/¾in) below the pot rim. Add or remove soil at the bottom if necessary. Once the level is correct, fill up the space around the root ball with more soil, firm it down with your hands as you go. Add more soil if necessary, until its level is just (2cm/¾in) below the pot rim. Then water in the shrub well. See also Looking after shrubs in containers, page 25.

1. Select a container that is at least twice the size of the pot in which your shrub (here *Salvia rosmarinus*/rosemary) is currently growing.
2. Position the container on feet or bricks before covering the drainage hole in the base with one or more crocks.
3. Add a layer of grit.
4. Half-fill the container with potting compost.
5. Insert the shrub so the top of the root ball is just below the container rim. Then backfill around the root ball with potting compost.
6. Lightly firm the potting compost with your hands.
7. Water the plant to settle it into the compost. Then leave it to establish in its new container.

Oregon grape

Mahonia aquifolium aka *Berberis aquifolium*

This small evergreen shrub produces spiny pinnate leaves, which initially are bronze-red; they then turn dark green in summer, and deep burgundy in autumn. In spring, fragrant, bright yellow flowers attract pollinators. They are followed by blue berries that are loved by birds and wildlife.

—

WHERE TO GROW

Oregon grape creates good ground cover and is ideal for a woodland garden planted en masse or used in a shady border. It does well in full or partial shade in humus-rich, moist but free-draining soil.

HOW TO GROW

Prune Oregon grape in spring after flowering, to keep it in shape, then apply a 10–15cm/4–6in layer of organic farmyard manure. See also Sawfly larvae, page 130.

GROWING TIP

To make more plants, collect and sow the seeds or strike semi-ripe cuttings (see page 32).

Family Berberidaceae	
Height and spread 0.5–1x1–1.5m/ 1½–3x3–5ft	
Habit Bushy	
Flowering time Spring	
Hardiness H5	
Position Partial shade– full shade	

ANTI-INFLAMMATORY
Oregon grape contains berberine, which is believed to reduce inflammatory skin conditions such as psoriasis. American-Indian peoples in the Pacific North-West used the plant as herbal medicine long before the Europeans arrived in the area.

NOTABLE CULTIVARS AND OTHER NOTABLE SPECIES

- 'Apollo' forms more compact ground cover with larger leaves, and its clusters of dark yellow, lightly scented flowers in spring are followed by bluish black berries.
- *M. japonica* (aka *Berberis japonica*) is an erect shrub with large, dark green, pinnate leaves and small, pale yellow flowers carried in sprays, in late winter, followed by blue-black berries.
- *M.* × *media* 'Winter Sun' is an upright shrub with long, spiny, dark green leaves and clusters of erect spikes bearing highly fragrant, yellow flowers in early winter.

Tree mallow 'Rosea'

Malva × clementii 'Rosea' aka *Lavatera × clementii* 'Rosea'

If you want a shrub that blooms continuously for months and is easy to grow, look no further; this mallow is the right candidate. It is a semi-evergreen subshrub that produces thousands of hollyhock-like, pink flowers from early summer, which enhances its greyish green foliage.

—

WHERE TO GROW

Plant in any well-drained soil in full sun. Avoid heavy wet ground. If your area is prone to frosts, plant 'Rosea' against a wall to protect it from cold drying winds.

HOW TO GROW

Once established, 'Rosea' is drought tolerant. Hard prune stems back to 30cm/12in in spring after all risk of frost has passed. Deadhead regularly to prolong flowering.

GROWING TIP

'Rosea' is a fast-growing shrub that will fill any gaps in your garden in no time. However, it is short-lived and usually becomes leggy, with fewer blooms, after five or six years, so propagate it by softwood cuttings in spring (see page 31).

Family Malvaceae

Height and spread 1.5–2.5x1.5–2.5m/ 5–8x5–8ft

Habit Bushy

Flowering time Summer

Hardiness H5

Position Sun

OTHER NOTABLE CULTIVARS

- 'Barnsley' produces masses of white flowers that turn pink when mature, and grey-green foliage.
- 'Mary Hope', to 1.2m/4ft tall, bears pink-white, saucer-shaped flowers with deep pink centres in summer.

KEW CREATION

'Kew Rose' was a seedling raised from *M. × clementii* 'Rosea' and is very similar to that cultivar. Both plants have pastel-green leaves and open pink flowers. However, it seems that 'Kew Rose' is more vigorous.

Great honey flower

Melianthus major

The imposing, bluish green foliage comprises large, evergreen, glaucous leaves with deeply toothed leaflets. From spring to summer, maroon-red spikes of honey-scented flowers emerge above the foliage. They are followed by pale brown seed pods.

WHERE TO GROW

For a tropical look in a garden (see Creating a jungle garden, page 72), plant in dry, light and free-draining soil in full sun, in a sheltered position where great honey flower has plenty of space to grow and to stand out.

HOW TO GROW

Water well until established. In early winter, apply a dry mulch (such as straw) around the base of the plant to protect it from frost damage. Propagate by softwood cuttings (see page 31).

GROWING TIP

Great honey flower responds well to hard pruning. If your plant has become too big, cut each stem back to two or three buds from the base, from where new growth will appear in spring.

Family Francoaceae	
Height and spread 1.5–2.5x1.5–2.5m/ 5–8x5–8ft	
Habit Bushy	
Flowering time Spring–summer	
Hardiness H3	
Position Sun	

NOTABLE CULTIVAR

- 'Purple Haze' has purple-tinged foliage, with deeply toothed leaflets, and small purple flowers in erect racemes in spring and summer.

DO NOT EAT
The native range for great honey flower is in the Cape Province of South Africa. On a sunny day there, the birds feast on the nectar dripping from the flowers, but no grazing animal will come close to the leaves as they are highly toxic and cause death in a few hours if ingested.

Common myrtle

Myrtus communis

Aromatic shiny leaves hung along copper-coloured stems adorn common myrtle. Its flowers are fluffy, white and fragrant, and cover this bushy evergreen shrub from mid- to late summer. They are followed in autumn by small, purple-black berries, which are a delight for birds.

—

WHERE TO GROW

It is an excellent shrub for a sunny sheltered position in poor, dry, free-draining soil, in a Mediterranean border or a gravel garden. In Mediterranean-type climates, common myrtle tolerates partial shade.

HOW TO GROW

Plant after the last frosts in spring, so common myrtle is protected from cold spells. In winter, apply a 10–15cm/4–6in layer of mulch such as straw or woody bark, to protect the roots from frost. Lightly prune by removing unwanted branches. Propagate by taking semi-ripe cuttings (see page 32).

GROWING TIP

You can plant common myrtle in a container. Choose a large one (40-litre) and place a 5–6cm/2–2½in layer of horticultural grit in the base of the container, to ensure excellent drainage, before filling the container with peat-free, multipurpose compost. Water well in summer. See also Growing a shrub in a container, page 96.

Family Myrtaceae

Height and spread
1.5–2.5x1.4–2.5m/
5–8x4½–8ft

Habit Bushy

Flowering time
Mid–late summer

Hardiness H4

Position Sun

NOTABLE SUBSPECIES

- subsp. *tarentina* has tiny, dark green leaves and large, pinkish white, fluffy flowers in summer, followed by white berries in autumn.

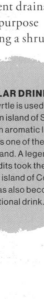

POPULAR DRINK
Common myrtle is used in the Mediterranean island of Sardinia to produce an aromatic liqueur called Mirto. It is one of the national drinks of the island. A legend is that Sardinian bandits took the liqueur to the nearby island of Corsica, where it has also become a traditional drink.

101

Heavenly bamboo

Nandina domestica

Heavenly bamboo is a small evergreen shrub grown for its impressive foliage colours. The young leaves are flushed with red in spring, mature to dark green in summer, and turn burgundy-red in autumn. Clusters of white flowers appear at the end of the branches in midsummer, and are followed by decorative, bright red berries in autumn.

—

WHERE TO GROW

Grow in fertile, moist but well-drained soil, sheltered from cold drying winds. The best foliage colours occur in full sun. Plant heavenly bamboo as a specimen plant in a shrub border, in a woodland setting or in an informal hedge (see Planting a hedge, page 126).

HOW TO GROW

Heavenly bamboo requires very little maintenance. Give it plenty of water until established. Keep pruning to a minimum by removing dead, weak or unwanted branches that spoil the symmetry of the plant. Propagate by taking semi-ripe cuttings (see page 32).

GROWING TIP

Keep your pets away from the berries as they are highly poisonous to all animals if ingested.

PLAIN CONFUSING

Despite its name, the heavenly bamboo is not related to bamboo plants. In fact, its closest cousin is *Berberis*. It is native to eastern Asia, the Himalayas and Japan, where inhabitants place the plant by their front doors to dispel bad dreams.

Family Berberidaceae	
Height and spread 1–1.5x1–1.5m/3–5x3–5ft	
Habit Bushy	
Flowering time Summer	
Hardiness H5	
Position Sun	

NOTABLE CULTIVARS

- 'Fire Power', to 60cm/24in tall, has ever-changing foliage colouring: the young, fuchsia-pink leaves turn bluish green in summer, and then deep burgundy-red and copper in autumn.
- 'Seika' is slow growing, with beautiful multicoloured foliage, offering hues of reds and pinks when young, blues and green in summer, and finally burgundy-reds in autumn.

Burkwood osmanthus

Osmanthus × burkwoodii

This hybrid osmanthus has a bushy rounded habit. In spring, the white flowers release a delicate, jasmine-like perfume. They are borne in clusters at the bases of the dark green, slightly toothed and leathery leaves. The shrub is evergreen and brings year-round interest in a garden.

—

WHERE TO GROW

Plant as a single specimen in a garden or in multiples in a hedge (see Planting a hedge, page 126). Burkwood osmanthus needs a sheltered position protected from cold winds, as well as rather light, fertile soil with good drainage. See also Planting a pot-grown shrub in the ground, page 104.

HOW TO GROW

Water well, once or twice a week, until the shrub is established, but make sure that the ground is not waterlogged. Trim only if needed, after flowering. Propagate by taking semi-ripe cuttings (see page 32).

GROWING TIP

Plant burkwood osmanthus in spring, to give it time to establish before winter. In frost-free climates, it can also be planted in autumn.

Family Oleaceae

Height and spread
2.5–4x2.5–4m/8–13x 8–13ft

Habit Bushy

Flowering time Spring

Hardiness H5

Position Sun–partial shade

NOTABLE SPECIES

- *O. delavayi* offers masses of highly scented, white flowers, in spring; it is evergreen with glossy, dark green leaves, finely toothed around the edges.
- *O. heterophyllus* 'Goshiki' (aka 'Tricolor') bears holly-like, pinkish bronze leaves when young, then within a few weeks they turn cream and gree,n producing a marble effect, which is best achieved in full sun.

MIXED ORIGINS

Osmanthus × burkwoodii is a hybrid created in 1924 at the English nursery Burkwood & Skipwith (hence the name). The parent plants are the Chinese *O. delavayi* and the Turkish *O. decorus*.

Planting a pot-grown shrub in the ground

Before going in the ground, a pot-grown shrub has spent its entire life in a container. Taking the plant out of a pot and putting it in the ground in what will be its permanent home can be a stressful change for the plant. Therefore, to give it a good start, it is important to follow some simple steps.

The best time to plant is in autumn in mild (frost-free) climates, or in spring in colder (frost-prone) regions. Shrubs of borderline hardiness should always be planted out in spring so they have many months to get established before the cold winter months.

Once you have watered the shrub and removed it from its container, gently loosen or straighten any roots that were circling the root ball. This will encourage them to grow outwards.

When you position the shrub in the planting hole, make sure it is straight and in the centre. Rotate it to get the most attractive side in full view. Then step back to get a better look.

It is very important to achieve the correct depth for the planting hole, so check by placing a stick or a plank across the hole – your shrub should be at the same level as it was in its pot. If the top of the root ball is too high, dig the hole a little bit more; if it is too low, add some soil to the bottom of the hole.

After planting, water thoroughly to saturate the root ball and surrounding soil. Continue to water the shrub in the following weeks and months. Do not let the soil dry out. See also Aftercare, page 24.

1   In the spot you have chosen for your shrub, remove all the weeds and larger stones. With a garden spade, dig a square hole about twice the width of the root ball and as deep as the pot the shrub is currently in.

2   Water the plant (here variegated holly olive/ *Osmanthus heterophyllus* 'Variegatus') thoroughly so the water reaches into the root ball. Then carefully remove the plant from its pot by placing one hand around the base of the branches while the other one pulls the pot away from the root ball.

3   Place the shrub in the prepared hole and check it is at the correct depth. Adjust the planting depth, if necessary, by removing or adding soil beneath the shrub.

4   Backfill around the shrub with the removed soil or with a mixture of one part compost to three parts soil if your soil is nutritionally poor. Using your hands or heels, firm it down as you go while holding the shrub upright and at the right depth and being careful not to touch the roots or root ball.

5   Once the shrub is firmly in place, water it generously and add more soil if you need to.

Mock orange 'Belle Étoile'

Philadelphus 'Belle Étoile'

Elegant arching branches bear a profusion of deliciously fragrant, large, single white flowers, tinged purple in the centre, in spring. They stand out beautifully against the deep green leaves. This shrub is deciduous.

WHERE TO GROW

Plant not too far from the house or the sitting area to enjoy the perfume. 'Belle Étoile' does well in all types of soil as long as it has good drainage. It can be part of an informal hedge (see Planting a hedge, page 126) or be planted singly in a garden.

HOW TO GROW

Water generously after planting until 'Belle Étoile' is well established. It is then resistant to summer droughts but prefers constant low moisture. Prune immediately after flowering, removing one-quarter of the older stems at ground level. Propagate by taking softwood cuttings (see page 31) or hardwood cuttings (see page 34).

GROWING TIP

In spring, apply a 10–15cm/ 4–6in layer of organic farmyard manure around the base of the plant, to encourage new healthy growth.

Family	Hydrangeaceae
Height and spread	1–1.5x1.5–2.5m/ 3–5x5–8ft
Habit	Bushy
Flowering time	Spring–summer
Hardiness	H6
Position	Sun–partial shade

OTHER SPECIES AND OTHER CULTIVARS

- *P. coronarius* 'Aureus' has brilliant golden yellow young foliage and fragrant, cup-shaped, creamy white flowers in summer.
- *P.* 'Manteau d'Hermine', to 75cm/30in tall, produces double, creamy white flowers with delicate orange-blossom perfume, in summer.
- *P.* 'Virginal', to 3m/10ft tall, has strong upright stems bearing highly fragrant, double, pure white flowers in summer.

PRAISED FOR ITS PERFUME

Mock orange flowers can easily fill the entire garden with their intoxicating fragrance, which is similar to that of an orange tree in full bloom but stronger and sweeter.

Christmas berry 'Red Robin'

Photinia × fraseri 'Red Robin'

The main attraction of this shrub is its shiny, parrot-red, young foliage that can be spotted from afar. If left unpruned, 'Red Robin' also produces frothy umbels of pale brown/creamy white flowers. It is evergreen, fast-growing and vigorous.

—

WHERE TO GROW

'Red Robin' is mostly planted as an evergreen hedge or screen (see Planting a hedge, page 126). It thrives in any well-drained soil and can withstand very cold temperatures. It can also be planted singly in a large container (see Growing a shrub in a container, page 96) or to hide a dull corner in the garden.

HOW TO GROW

Water well for the first two years after planting, especially in summer if the weather is dry. Once established, 'Red Robin' tolerates periods of drought. Propagate by taking semi-ripe cuttings (see page 32).

GROWING TIP

Prune in summer by cutting all the branches by half. This encourages the growth of new red leaves in autumn without compromising the flowers in spring.

Family Rosaceae	
Height and spread 2.5–4 x 2.5–4m/8–13 x 8–13ft	
Habit Bushy	
Flowering time Spring	
Hardiness H5	
Position Sun–partial shade	

ANOTHER NOTABLE CULTIVAR

- 'Little Red Robin', to 1m/3ft tall, has parrot-red young leaves maturing to dark green; it usually bears creamy white flowers in sunny conditions in spring.

NAMES EXPLAINED

The Greek word for 'shiny' is *photeinos*, which probably references the glossy leaves in the genus *Photinia*. *Fraseri* comes from the Fraser nursery in Alabama, USA, where this cross between *Photinia serratifolia* and *P. glabra* originates. Finally, the cultivar name 'Red Robin' was designated by a New Zealand grower.

Pieris 'Forest Flame'

Pieris 'Forest Flame'

This shrub is grown for its colour-changing foliage. The young red leaves turn coral-pink, then creamy white and finally dark green in summer. In spring, it produces clusters of ivory, bell-like flowers, which resemble those of lily of the valley (*Convallaria majalis*) and attract bees and other insects.

—

WHERE TO GROW

Choose a position in acidic, moist but free-draining soil in a shrub border or at a woodland edge shaded from the morning sun. 'Forest Flame' also thrives in a container filled with ericaceous compost (see also Growing a shrub in a container, page 96).

HOW TO GROW

'Forest Flame' is relatively easy to grow as long as the soil is appropriate. Apply a 10–15cm/4–6in layer of ericaceous compost around the base of the plant in early spring, to improve the soil. Pruning is not recommended. Propagate by taking semi-ripe cuttings (see page 32).

GROWING TIP

If you have access to pine needles, use them to replace the ericaceous compost as a soil improver in spring; they will also keep the soil around the plant moist in summer.

FLORAL TRIBUTE

Pieris is sometimes referred to as the lily of the valley tree because of its pure white flowers, which look very much like those of lily of the valley.

Family	Ericaceae
Height and spread	2.5–4x1.5–2.5m/ 8–13x5–8ft
Habit	Bushy
Flowering time	Spring
Hardiness	H5
Position	Sun–partial shade

NOTABLE SPECIES AND CULTIVARS

- *P. japonica* 'Katsura', to 1.5m/5ft tall, produces impressive, mahogany-red new growth and clusters of pink and white flowers in early spring.
- *P. japonica* 'Little Heath', to 60cm/24in tall, has pale green leaves edged with creamy white, and clusters of pink buds opening into white, bell-like flowers, in spring.
- *P. japonica* 'Mountain Fire' bears brilliant red young leaves turning chestnut-brown then dark green; in spring, it carries clusters of ivory-coloured, bell-like flowers.

Tawhiwhi

Pittosporum tenuifolium

Tawhiwhi is mainly chosen for its evergreen foliage and for providing a permanent structure to a garden in a relatively short time. Its shiny, wavy-edged leaves contrast nicely with its black stems. Tiny, deep purple, fragrant flowers open in clusters in spring and summer.

—

WHERE TO GROW

Being very versatile, tawhiwhi does well in an urban or coastal garden, in a bed or border or as an informal hedge (see Planting a hedge, page 126). Plant in a fertile, moist but well-drained soil, somewhere sheltered from cold and drying winds.

HOW TO GROW

When planting, mix the garden soil with two large handfuls each of leafmould and horticultural sand. Give the shrub plenty of water until well established. Pruning is not necessary unless you want to trim your plant to form a ball or a hedge. Propagate by taking semi-ripe cuttings (see page 32).

GROWING TIP

When tawhiwhi has grown enough in size, you can remove the lower branches to make a standard tree.

NATURAL FRAGRANCE

In its native New Zealand, the gum of tawhiwhi, kōhūhū and kōhūkōhū (all Māori names for pittosporum) was a key ingredient in the manufacture of many Māori perfume recipes.

Family	Pittosporaceae
Height and spread	4–8x2.5–4m/13–26x 8–13ft
Habit	Bushy
Flowering time	Spring–summer
Hardiness	H4
Position	Sun–partial shade

NOTABLE CULTIVARS

- 'Golf Ball', to 1m/3ft tall, develops dense foliage and a rounded shape, which are ideal for a topiary ball.
- 'Irene Paterson', to 1.5m/5ft tall, has almost white, young leaves becoming green blotched with creamy white.
- 'Tom Thumb', to 1m/3ft tall, produces dark brown stems and small, dark purple, mature leaves, which contrast beautifully with its fresh green leaves.
- *P.* 'Garnettii' has black stems and grey-green leaves edged with cream, sometimes tinted pink in winter.

Firethorn Saphyr Orange

Pyracantha Saphyr Orange ('Cadange') aka *P.* 'Orange Cadence'

This thorny evergreen shrub is both incredibly robust and ornamental. In spring and summer, small white flowers emerge from among the dark green leaves and, in autumn, they are followed by masses of bright orange berries. Not only do these bring a blaze of colour to a garden but they are also a feast for birds at a time when bright colours and food are most needed.

WHERE TO GROW

Use as a hedge to deter any intruder from passing through and also to provide shelter for wildlife, or plant Saphyr Orange with other firethorn varieties to create a colourful combination. When grown as a free-standing shrub, it lightens up a border or dull wall. See also Planting a hedge, page 126.

HOW TO GROW

Water well for the first two years after planting. Once established, Saphyr Orange is very resistant to summer drought. Propagate by taking semi-ripe cuttings (see page 32).

GROWING TIP

Prune lightly after flowering, wearing thick gloves and long sleeves as the thorns are terribly prickly.

Family Rosaceae	
Height and spread 1.5–2.5x1.5–2.5m/ 5–8x5–8ft	
Habit Bushy	
Flowering time Spring–summer	
Hardiness H6	
Position Sun–partial shade	

NOTABLE CULTIVARS

- Saphyr Jaune ('Cadaune') has dark green leaves and masses of bright yellow berries in autumn.
- Saphyr Rouge ('Cadrou') produces dark green leaves and masses of bright orange-red berries in autumn.

BEWARE OF PUNCTURES

The sharp thorns of firethorn can cut and poke holes in skin. Although they are not considered toxic, the skin around the puncture can become red, swollen, painful and itchy.

Rhododendron 'Cunningham's White'

Rhododendron 'Cunningham's White'

There are many great cultivars of rhododendron, not only within the large-leaved, large-flowering, hardy rhododendrons but also among the rather smaller azaleas, which are also in the same genus. 'Cunningham's White' is a robust evergreen shrub with deep green leaves and loose trusses of funnel-shaped, white flowers flushed with gold in their centres.

—

WHERE TO GROW

Grow in a border only if you have acidic soil. Find a sheltered position in humus-rich, moist but well-drained soil in partial shade or sun, at the edge of a woodland border. Otherwise, grow it in a container filled with ericaceous compost.

HOW TO GROW

Plant it so the roots are just below the soil's surface – never any deeper. Water with rainwater if possible. Deadhead the spent flowers; any other pruning is not recommended. Propagate by taking semi-ripe cuttings (see page 32) or by simple layering (see page 35).

GROWING TIP

When 'Cunningham's White' is grown in a pot, make sure it has plenty of drainage holes (see Growing a shrub in a container, page 96). Keep it moist and cool in partial shade. Every spring, replace the top layer of soil with fresh ericaceous compost, or repot completely.

Family Ericaceae	
Height and spread 1.5–2.5x2.5–4m/ 5–8x8–13ft	
Habit Bushy	
Flowering time Spring	
Hardiness H6	
Position Sun–partial shade	

NOTABLE CULTIVARS

- *R.* 'Blue Danube' (evergreen azalea), to 70cm/28in tall, bears large, violet-blue flowers in late spring and small, emerald-green leaves.
- *R* 'Dreamland' (hybrid rhododendron) carries large, pastel-pink flowers, which are loved by bees, in late spring or early summer, and dark green leaves with pale undersides.
- *R.* 'Mother's Day' (evergreen azalea), to 80cm/32in tall, has masses of small, bright red flowers in late spring and early summer, and small, dark green leaves.

LASTING LEGACY

In 1847, Sir Joseph Hooker became the first European to explore the northern state of India that was then the autonomous kingdom of Sikkim. During a four-year-long, perilous expedition, Hooker discovered many species of *Rhododendron* and brought young plants and seeds to the Royal Botanic Gardens, Kew, where they were planted in the hollow walk, known today as the Rhododendron Dell. Some of Hooker's specimens are still there.

Making rosemary and lavender soap

Soaps are very easy to find in stores but they are not always gentle on the skin and often contain chemicals and artificial scents. Making your soap at home will allow you to control its composition and adapt the ingredients according to your needs. In addition, you will be able to personalize it with your favourite fragrances or make it into an original shape.

The fastest way to make soap is to use vegetable glycerine or ready-made soap paste to which you add a mix of seeds (such as aniseed or flax seeds), dried flowers, essential oils and fragrances. One of each of these ingredients is enough as you don't want to put too many in your soap. For this project, I chose rosemary (*Salvia rosmarinus*) leaves and lavender (*Lavandula*) flowers as they both have a stimulating effect on the skin. They also have antiseptic and anti-inflammatory properties. As optional extras, I included African marigolds (*Tagetes erecta*) and globe amaranth (*Gomphrena globosa*). However, any other aromatic leaves or dried petals will work as well. The combinations are endless.

You will need

- Fresh rosemary leaves
- Dried lavender flowers
- Bowl
- Kettle
- Saucepan
- Ready-made soap paste
- Sieve
- Dried African marigold petals
- Dried globe amaranth flowers
- Pure organic lavender essential oil
- Citronella essential oil
- Long-handled spoon
- Multi-celled silicon mould

1 Choose a dry sunny day to harvest rosemary leaves in the garden.
2 Gather the ingredients and materials you want to use for your soap.
3 Place the lavender flowers and rosemary leaves in a bowl and pour a cup of steaming hot water over them. Allow to infuse for ten minutes.
4 In a saucepan, melt the ready-made soap paste over low heat.
5 Strain the rosemary and lavender infusion and add this liquid into the melted soap paste. Add all the other ingredients. Stir until blended.
6 Pour the mix into the cells in the mould and let it cool down at room temperature, until hardened.
7 Once cooled, remove the soaps from the mould. Store them in a cupboard or wrap them in craft paper to gift to family and friends.

Flowering currant

Ribes sanguineum

The flowering currant is a vigorous deciduous shrub, which is naturally multi-stemmed with an upright arching habit. Its aromatic, dark green leaves emerge in spring at the same time as the flowers. These are dark pink – almost red – tubular and very abundant. They are followed by dark purple berries, which birds and small mammals feast on.

—

WHERE TO GROW

Plant in moderately fertile, well-drained soil, in any garden, as an informal hedge (see Planting a hedge, page 126), in a shrub border or as a specimen plant. It can also be grown in a container (see Growing a shrub in a container, page 96). Although a sun lover, flowering currant prefers partial shade if the sun is unusually strong.

HOW TO GROW

When planting, backfill with a mix of equal parts of organic garden compost and soil. Water regularly until the plant is established, but make sure that the soil is not waterlogged. Propagate by taking hardwood cuttings (see page 34).

GROWING TIP

Prune immediately after flowering by cutting back flowered stems to strong young shoots lower down. Also, cut out one in five ageing stems near the base.

Family Grossulariaceae	
Height and spread 1.5–2.5x1.5–2.5m/ 5–8x5–8ft	
Habit Upright, arching	
Flowering time Spring	
Hardiness H6	
Position Sun–partial shade	

TRUE COMPETITOR

Gooseberries are also part of the *Ribes* genus and were extremely fashionable in nineteenth-century England, which saw the emergence of many 'gooseberry clubs'. These clubs organized annual competitions during which prizes were offered for the largest, the smoothest or the most flavourful gooseberry.

NOTABLE CULTIVARS AND OTHER NOTABLE SPECIES

- 'Elkington's White' is thornless and produces pendent clusters of white tubular flowers in spring, followed by small, blue-black berries in summer.
- 'King Edward VII' has aromatic foliage and deep red flowers in drooping racemes in spring, followed by black berries in summer.
- *R. odoratum* (aka *R. aureum* var. *villosum*) is also thornless, with fragrant yellow flowers in spring, then black berries; its bright green leaves turn red and purple in autumn.

Russian sage 'Blue Spire'

Salvia 'Blue Spire' aka *Perovskia* 'Blue Spire'

From midsummer to early autumn, little lilac-blue flowers are borne on grey-green spikes above the main framework of the shrub and look like a light blue cloud floating above the border. The foliage is deciduous and composed of finely cut, aromatic leaves.

—

WHERE TO GROW

Grow in poor sandy soil in a dry garden, whether planted as single shrubs or in clusters of three or five to intensify the 'blue cloud' effect. Good drainage is essential.

HOW TO GROW

Maintain by shortening the stems to 10cm/4in above ground level, in early spring.

GROWING TIP

To make more plants, propagate Russian sage by softwood cuttings in late spring (see page 31) or by semi-ripe cuttings in summer (see page 32).

Family Lamiaceae

Height and spread 1–1.5x0.5–1m/3–5x 1½–3ft

Habit Bushy

Flowering time Midsummer–early autumn

Hardiness H5

Position Sun

ANOTHER NOTABLE CULTIVAR

- 'Little Spire' (aka *Perovskia* 'Little Spire'), to 60cm/24in tall, has shorter stems than 'Blue Spire' so does not flop.

TAXONOMISTS, THANK YOU

The sage that then wasn't a sage is now a sage again and is not from Russia (but native to the steppes and hills of south-western and central Asia) ..., Russian sage is a plant whose name spells trouble. Having been known at one time as *Perovskia atriplicifolia* it has been recently reclassified and is now *Salvia yangii*. The most common cultivar 'Blue Spire' could be a hybrid and is named *Salvia* 'Blue Spire' by the Royal Horticultural Society.

Rosemary

Salvia rosmarinus aka *Rosmarinus officinalis*

This renowned Mediterranean shrub is grown for its aromatic edible leaves and spikes of violet-blue flowers. The linear evergreen leaves are grey-green with white undersides, giving the shrub a silvery appearance.

—

WHERE TO GROW

Rosemary grows best on poor dry soil and is therefore ideal for a dry garden, a Mediterranean border or a pot on a patio or balcony. Place it in a sunny position near the house or a seating area where you can enjoy its perfume.

HOW TO GROW

Being easy to grow, rosemary does not need any specific care. Prune in spring after flowering, if necessary, to encourage bushy growth and to maintain shape.

GROWING TIP

Semi-ripe cuttings taken between late summer and mid-autumn are an easy way to propagate rosemary (see page 32).

Family	Lamiaceae
Height and spread	1.5–2.5x1.5–2.5m/ 5–8x5–8ft
Habit	Bushy
Flowering time	Spring–summer
Hardiness	H4
Position	Sun

FAMOUS WATER
Rosemary is the subject of many legends. One of them is that Elisabeth of Poland, Queen of Hungary, retained her youthful beauty at the age of seventy-two, thanks to the famous Hungarian Water made using rosemary. Another beauty tip is to use rosemary leaves for home-made soap (see Making rosemary and lavender soap, page 112).

NOTABLE CULTIVARS

- Albiflora Group (white rosemary) produces masses of sweetly scented, white flowers in late spring and summer.
- 'Miss Jessopp's Upright' is vigorous, with purple-blue flowers and very fine leaves.

Elder

Sambucus nigra

Many people enjoy the refreshing summer drink made of elder flowers (see also Home-made elderflower cordial, page 118). Large, flat, creamy white blooms emerge in early summer. They are followed by edible (when cooked) black berries. The green pinnate leaves are deciduous.

—

WHERE TO GROW

Plant in any well-drained, humus-rich soil, in sun or partial shade. Elder is particularly suitable for informal flowering hedges (see Planting a hedge, page 126) and for 'wild' gardens.

HOW TO GROW

Being easy to grow, elder requires little care. In early spring, before the flowers appear, cut any dead, damaged and crossing branches as well as any other shoots that compromise the symmetry of the shrub. Propagate by softwood cuttings (see page 31) or hardwood cuttings (see page 34).

GROWING TIP

Elder tolerates hard pruning but make sure that it receives a 10–15cm/4–6in layer of well-rotted manure afterwards.

Family Viburnaceae

Height and spread 4–8x2.5–4m/13–26x 8–13ft

Habit Open

Flowering time Early summer

Hardiness H6

Position Sun–partial shade

NOTABLE FORM AND ANOTHER NOTABLE SPECIES

- f. *porphyrophylla* 'Eva' produces black foliage and flat umbels of pink flowers followed by little black berries.
- *S. racemosa* 'Sutherland Gold' carries golden leaves, creamy white flowers and glossy red berries.

WIDESPREAD
Native to the UK, elder can be seen all over the country growing in woodland, scrub, wasteland and along hedgerows.

Home-made elderflower cordial

Elderflower cordial is a fragrant and refreshing drink, which is excellent at quenching thirst in the torpor of summer days and nights. Home-made cordial tastes much better than the ones sold in shops. Fortunately, it is simple to make and needs only a few ingredients. The satisfaction you will derive from tasting your own drink will mean that you are unlikely ever to buy supermarket cordial again.

On a bright dry morning in early summer, look for elder (*Sambucus nigra*, see page 117) trees in any area that is not too close to a busy road and from them pick good-quality flower heads that are well out of the reach of dogs or foxes. Two large handfuls of flower heads should suffice. Go home straight afterwards, as the cordial should be made within a few hours of collecting the elder flowers.

You will need

- 20–30 elderflower heads
- Secateurs
- Clean tea towel
- Bowl
- Kettle
- Kitchen paper
- Fine-mesh sieve
- Large saucepan
- 3 unwaxed lemons, juiced (without seeds)
- 5 cups of white granulated sugar
- Washed and sterilized glass bottles
- Funnel

1. Cut the flower heads carefully, with clean secateurs, without damaging the rest of each branch. Do not wash the flower heads.
2. Set the flower heads in a bowl or on a clean tea towel for a couple of hours, to allow any insects to escape.
3. Remove the stalks from the flower heads, and place the flowers in a bowl. Pour 1.5 litres/2½ pints of boiling water over the flowers, cover with a tea towel or similar and leave to infuse overnight.
4. The next day, strain the elderflower infusion through the sieve into the saucepan. Add the lemon juice.
5. Simmer over low heat. Add the sugar and stir until it's dissolved. Bring the liquid to a boil, then reduce the heat and simmer for ten minutes.
6. Pour the liquid into the glass bottle, using the funnel if necessary. Allow to cool. You can use the cordial straight away diluted with sparkling water or lemonade.

Cotton lavender

Santolina chamaecyparissus aka lavender cotton

A soft mound of finely cut, silvery leaves, very aromatic
when crushed, forms on this evergreen Mediterranean shrub.
In summer, small, bright yellow, button-like flowers are borne
at the ends of the wiry stems. Just like lavender (*Lavandula*; see
page 90) cotton lavender evokes sunny Italy and the north-west
Balkan Peninsula, where it is native.

—

WHERE TO GROW

Grow in perfectly well-drained or dry, poor, stony or sandy
soil in full sun, even in a spot exposed to scorching midday sun.
Use as ground cover in a gravel garden, a rock garden or in front
of a Mediterranean border.

HOW TO GROW

Cotton lavender needs very little care and maintenance.
Prune just after flowering, to keep the beautiful, naturally
rounded shape, or earlier, just before flowering if the
flowers are undesirable. Propagate by taking semi-ripe
cuttings (see page 32).

GROWING TIP

This shrub thrives in a pot in full sun,
but make sure that you water it only
when the soil is completely dry all
the way down.

Family	Asteraceae
Height and spread	10–50x50–100cm/ 4–20x20–39in
Habit	Rounded
Flowering time	Summer
Hardiness	H5
Position	Sun

ANOTHER NOTABLE SPECIES

- *S. rosmarinifolia* 'Lemon Fizz' forms a dense bushy mound with bright lemon-yellow flowers that rises above bright lemon-green, finely cut, aromatic leaves in summer.

PEST REPELLENT
Victorian gardeners often
planted cotton lavender in
a kitchen garden border to
discourage cabbage white
butterflies and other predatory
insects from feasting on
the vegetables.

Sweet box

Sarcococca confusa

From early winter until early spring, sweet box produces pure white, tiny flowers. Their sweet and heavy fragrance perfumes the whole garden with vanilla. These blooms are followed by rounded black berries. The foliage is evergreen with shiny, deep green leaves.

Family Buxaceae	
Height and spread 1–1.5x1–1.5m/3–5x3–5ft	
Habit Bushy	
Flowering time Early winter–early spring	
Hardiness H5	
Position Partial shade– full shade	

WHERE TO GROW

Plant in moist but free-draining soil in shade. Sweet box is best positioned close to the house where you can enjoy its perfume. It is also great under a deciduous tree, or in a container for the terrace or the balcony (see Growing a shrub in a container, page 96).

HOW TO GROW

Lightly prune after flowering, to maintain a nice shape. Apply a 10–15cm/4–6in layer of organic farmyard manure around the base of the plant in spring. Propagate by taking semi-ripe cuttings (see page 32).

GROWING TIP

Sweet box is an excellent plant for challenging conditions such as dry soil or deep shade, a cool border or woodland understorey. It also tolerates urban pollution.

EXPEDITION FIND
The first *Sarcococca* – *Sarcococca hookeriana* var. *hookeriana* – to be introduced into English gardens was discovered by Sir Joseph Hooker (Director of the Royal Botanic Gardens, Kew) during his mid-nineteenth-century expedition to a remote region in the northern Himalayas.

ANOTHER NOTABLE SPECIES

- *S. hookeriana* var. *digyna* 'Purple Stem' has rather narrow, mid- to dark green leaves, on dark purple stems, and highly fragrant, white flowers flushed pink at their bases.
- *S. hookeriana* var. *humilis*, to 60cm/24in tall and 90cm/36in wide, bears narrowly lanced-shaped, dark green leaves and pink-flushed, white flowers, scented with notes of honey and vanilla, followed by long-lasting, black berries.

Japanese skimmia

Skimmia japonica

Bright red, ornamental berries, on female plants, persist all through winter so this is very good shrub for a shady spot in a winter garden. It is evergreen with a compact rounded habit and dark green, aromatic leaves. Dark red buds are produced in autumn and last until the creamy white flowers open in spring, at the tips of the branches.

—

WHERE TO GROW

Plant in humus-rich, light, moist but well-drained soil in partial or full shade, protected from cold drying winds. Japanese skimmia is also useful in a woodland border or in a container on a patio (see Growing a shrub in a container, page 96).

HOW TO GROW

Apply a 10–15cm/4–6in layer of acidic mulch once a year. Also ensure Japanese skimmia has enough water for the soil not to dry out for too long. Pruning is not necessary. Propagate by taking softwood cuttings (see page 31) or semi-ripe cuttings (see page 32).

GROWING TIP

Avoid calcareous dry alkaline soils as well as heavy soils as they may cause chlorosis and brown spots on leaves.

KEW CULTIVARS FOR BERRIES
Plant male *S. × confusa* 'Kew Green' next to female *S. japonica* 'Kew White' if you want to enjoy beautiful, snow-white berries in autumn.

Family	Rutaceae
Height and spread	1.5–2.5x1–1.5m/ 5–8x3–5ft
Habit	Rounded
Flowering time	Spring
Hardiness	H5
Position	Partial shade– full shade

NOTABLE CULTIVARS AND NOTABLE HYBRID

- *S. × confusa* 'Kew Green' (male), to 1m/3ft tall, bears aromatic leaves and large clusters of yellow-green flowers in spring and summer.
- 'Kew White' (female) produces clusters of white flowers in spring, followed by masses of snow-white berries if a male skimmia is growing nearby.
- 'Rubella' (male) has dense evergreen foliage, and in autumn it produces dark red flower buds, which open to fragrant white flowers in spring.

Japanese spiraea

Spiraea japonica

The Japanese spiraea is a large, bushy, deciduous shrub with lance-shaped, bright green leaves. In summer, sprays of white or pink flowers appear at the tips of the dark stems, making a stunning contrast with the foliage. They are followed by small capsules that contain seeds.

WHERE TO GROW

Grow in any fertile, moist but well-drained soil. Japanese spiraea prefers full sun but tolerates partial shade. Use as a low hedge (see Planting a hedge, page 126), as a permanent structure in a perennial bed or as ground cover in a large sunny border.

HOW TO GROW

Water well the first year after planting. Hard prune stems, in early spring, back to 10–15cm/4–6in above ground level, to encourage more blooms the following year. After that, apply a 10–15cm/4–6in layer of organic farmyard manure around the base of the plant. Propagate by taking softwood cuttings (see page 31), semi-ripe cuttings (see page 32) or hardwood cuttings (see page 34).

GROWING TIP

Deadhead the spent flowers to keep your shrub looking good and to encourage more blooms.

Family Rosaceae	
Height and spread 1–1.5x1–1.5m/3–5x3–5ft	
Habit Bushy	
Flowering time Summer	
Hardiness H6	
Position Sun–partial shade	

NOTABLE CULTIVARS AND ANOTHER NOTABLE SPECIES

- 'Firelight' produces bright orange, young leaves turning golden yellow then green before taking on vibrant autumn colours; its flowers are fluffy and deep pink.
- *S.* 'Arguta', to 2.5m/8ft tall and wide, has soft green, narrow leaves and sprays of tiny white flowers on gracefully arching branches.
- *S. nipponica* 'Snowmound', to 2.5m/8ft tall, has arching branches bearing large clusters of tiny, bowl-shaped, white flowers, which are very attractive to bees and other pollinating insects.

ASPIRIN
The letters 'spir' within the word 'aspirin' reflect the fact that this medicinal drug contains *Spiraea*. In fact, for thousands of years people used to chew spiraea's bark – which contains salicylic acid – to ease their aches and pain. The tea made from the bark was believed to reduce fevers.

Common lilac

Syringa vulgaris

One of the most effective deciduous flowering shrubs is common lilac, which is popular for its abundant and wonderfully fragrance blooms, borne in long panicles in spring and summer. These purple, pink or white blooms are perfect for cut flowers. Many common lilacs develop into small trees.

—

WHERE TO GROW

Plant in fertile, humus-rich and free-draining soil near a path, where you can enjoy the perfume. Lilac thrives in full sun but not in Mediterranean-type climates as it needs the chills of winter to form flowering buds.

HOW TO GROW

Being easy to grow, common lilac requires little maintenance except for plenty of water in dry weather. Immediately after flowering, remove the faded flowers carefully to avoid damaging new buds. Propagate by taking softwood cuttings (see page 31).

GROWING TIP

Remove root suckers that form at the base of the plant if you want common lilac to develop into a small tree rather than a shrub (see page 27).

Family Oleaceae	
Height and spread 4–8x4–8m/13–26x 13–26ft	
Habit Bushy	
Flowering time Spring–summer	
Hardiness H6	
Position Sun	

NOTABLE CULTIVARS

- 'Madame Lemoine' has soft green, heart-shaped leaves covered with large panicles of highly fragrant, double, white flowers from late spring to early summer.
- *S. meyeri* 'Palibin', to 1.5m/5ft tall and wide, bears dark green, oval leaves and fragrant, purple-pink flowers from late spring to early summer.
- *S.* 'Red Pixie', to 1.8m/6ft tall, carries small, soft green leaves, with purple leaf stalks, and red buds opening into fragrant, pale pink flowers in summer.

SYMBOL OF LOVE

The lilac is one of two official flowers associated with a couple's eighth wedding anniversary.

Rakai hebe

Veronica rakaiensis aka *Hebe rakaiensis*

The rakai hebe is a compact evergreen shrub, which forms a very neat, little dome of tiny, bright green leaves. In summer, the short spikes of white flowers attract bees and butterflies (see also Building a butterfly house, page 48). Small-leaved hebe such as rakai hebe are hardier and more resistant to hot dry weather than large-leaved hebes.

—

WHERE TO GROW

Grow in any soil, even poor, provided that it is very well-drained. Rakai hebe does well in a pot (see Growing a shrub in a container, page 96) or planted in numbers as a low formal hedge along the front of a border, preferably in a sunny position (see Planting a hedge, page 126). See also Creating a jungle garden, page 72.

HOW TO GROW

Plant in spring, and water until well established. Make sure that the water drains well, especially if your hebe is in a pot. Propagate by taking semi-ripe cuttings (see page 32).

GROWING TIP

Pruning is not necessary but you may want to keep the shape of your plant especially if it is grown as a hedge. In this case, lightly prune unsightly shoots in spring, making sure that you do not cut into old wood.

Family Plantaginaceae

Height and spread 0.5–1x1–1.5m/1½–3x 3–5ft

Habit Bushy

Flowering time Summer

Hardiness H4

Position Sun–partial shade

OTHER NOTABLE SPECIES AND CULTIVARS

- *V. albicans* (aka *Hebe albicans*) has dense foliage of tiny, glaucous blue-green leaves and pink-flushed buds that open to bright white flowers in early summer.
- *V.* 'Emerald Gem' (aka *Hebe* 'Emerald Gem') grows into a perfectly clean and tidy little green ball and carries small white flowers in summer.
- *V.* 'Frozen Flame' (aka *Hebe* 'Frozen Flame') produces variegated foliage that turns pinkish purple in winter as well as spikes of blue flowers in midsummer.

WHAT DOES IT MEAN?
Rakai hebe is native to the South Island of New Zealand. It seems that the name 'rakai' is of Māori origin and it could mean 'The light that shines around an angel'.

Planting a hedge

Pride is what you should feel once you have planted a hedge instead of erecting a wooden fence or a brick wall. You will certainly require a little bit more patience to obtain complete privacy and protection, but Mother Nature will be extremely grateful to you for your decision. By not using harsh landscaping materials, you will have avoided adding carbon emissions into the atmosphere. Another bonus is that your new hedge will actually capture carbon. A hedge provides shelter, food and a breeding site for wildlife such as nesting birds. In cities in particular, a hedge is a safe green corridor for animals to migrate from one area to another. Once your hedge has grown into the desired size, you will appreciate its many advantages, and so will the small creatures that are increasingly in distress with the changing climate. Before doing anything else, first talk to your neighbours about your plan if you are planting a hedge along your joint boundary. Then decide on which type of hedging plants (traditional evergreen, low hedge, flowering hedge) you want and how many plants you need (see Shrubs for hedges, page 17).

The best time to plant your hedge is in autumn. However, pot-grown plants can be planted at any time of year provided the soil is not frozen or waterlogged and the weather not too dry. Water your new hedge regularly until it is well established (at least two years). Once a year, feed the hedge with a general-purpose fertilizer (using the quantities recommended on the packaging) and apply a 10–15cm/4–6in layer of mulch. Remove the weeds on both sides of the hedge regularly.

1 A month or so before receiving your hedging plants, mark the planting line for your hedge with string secured between two sticks. Then prepare the ground by removing all weeds 30cm/12in on both sides of the proposed planting line.

2 Dig a series of holes or a trench 45–60cm/18–24in wide. Add a 10cm/4in layer of good-quality organic farmyard manure at the bottom. Leave it to rest.

3 As soon as your hedging plants arrive, water them thoroughly. Then remove the plants (here, silverthorn/ *Elaeagnus pungens* and *Forsythia × intermedia*) from their pots or any other wrappings, and place them into the holes or trench, at their correct spacings, with the top of each root ball at the same level as the surrounding soil.

4 Backfill the holes or trench. Mix in one part garden compost to three parts soil if you have sandy or clay soils.

5 As you fill the holes or trench, firm the soil with your heel. Water each plant well (a full bucket or watering can per plant).

6 Mulch with bark chips to reduce weed growth and keep the moisture in.

Laurustinus

Viburnum tinus

This winter- and spring-flowering, evergreen shrub produces clusters of tiny, fragrant, pinkish white flowers, which are an invaluable source of nectar for pollinating insects. The dark blue berries then provide food for robins and finches. The leaves are oval, dark green and glossy.

—

WHERE TO GROW

Plant versatile laurustinus in a moderately fertile, moist but well-drained soil in a group as an informal hedge (see Planting a hedge, page 126), or solitary as a specimen shrub in a border or in a large container (see Growing a shrub in a container, page 96). It tolerates a wide range of light conditions, including full shade

HOW TO GROW

Prune only to remove dead, diseased or unsightly branches. This must be done after flowering. Propagate by taking semi-hardwood cuttings (see page 34).

GROWING TIP

Do not deadhead the spent flowers so the shrub can produce its beautiful berries.

Family Viburnaceae

Height and spread 2.5–4x2.5–4m/8–13x 8–13ft

Habit Bushy

Flowering time Winter–spring

Hardiness H4

Position Sun–full shade

NOTABLE CULTIVAR AND OTHER NOTABLE SPECIES

- *V. × bodnantense* 'Dawn' is deciduous and grown for its fragrant, pink, virtually sterile flowers on bare stems.
- *V. davidii*, to 1.5m/5ft tall and wide, has dark green, ribbed, evergreen leaves and turquoise-blue berries (on female plants) on bright red stems.

- 'Eve Price' produces clusters of tiny white flowers opening from deep pink buds; they are followed by metallic blue-black berries.
- *V. opulus* 'Roseum', to 5m/16ft tall, is deciduous, bears snowball-like clusters of creamy white sterile flowers and fresh green leaves that turn purple in autumn.

FRAGRANT BURKWOODII

This cross between *V. utile* and *V. carlesii* was created by the Burkwood brothers Arthur and Albert in their nursery in Kingston-upon-Thames, UK. The shrub bears wonderfully scented, pinkish white flowers, which appear in rounded clusters in spring and fill the air with the most delicious perfume.

Weigela

Weigela florida

Weigela is a hardy deciduous shrub. From late spring to early summer, masses of pale pink, trumpet flowers are borne in clusters at the end of gracefully arching branches. The leaves are ovate, dark green and rather small.

—

WHERE TO GROW

Plant in any fertile, moist but well-drained soil as a specimen in a border, in front of a sunny wall or in small groups for hedging or a screen (see Planting a hedge, page 126). Weigela prefers a sunny position but tolerates some shade,

HOW TO GROW

Prune after flowering by removing dead, diseased and crossing branches right down to the base. Also cut back the flowered stems to below the spent flowers.

GROWING TIP

Propagate by softwood cuttings in early summer (see page 31), semi-ripe cuttings in midsummer (see page 32) or hardwood cuttings in late autumn or winter (see page 34).

Family Caprifoliaceae

Height and spread 1.5–2.5x1.5–2.5m/ 5–8x5–8ft

Habit Arching

Flowering time Late spring–early summer

Hardiness H6

Position Sun–partial shade

NOTABLE CULTIVARS AND ANOTHER NOTABLE SPECIES

- *W.* 'Bristol Ruby' produces masses of deep red, trumpet flowers in late spring and early summer.
- *W.* 'Florida Variegata' has variegated leaves, dark green in their centres and creamy white around the edges; the trumpet-shaped, deep pink, young flowers turn paler when mature.
- *W. middendorffiana* bears bright green leaves and pale yellow, trumpet-shaped flowers.

OLD FRIEND
Weigela florida was the first weigela species to be introduced into European gardens in the nineteenth century from its native Korea, northern China, Japan and Manchuria. Here, *florida* is from the Latin meaning 'many flowers' and does not refer to Florida in the USA.

Troubleshooting

Given the right growing conditions, a shrub can thrive happily for many years without too many troubles. Although shrubs are usually more resistant to pests and diseases than plants such as roses or vegetables, this doesn't mean that they are invulnerable. Extreme weather and physical damage can cause a lot of stress to a plant, which then becomes less resistant to pests and diseases.

Shrubs are particularly vulnerable between the moment they have been planted and the time they are well established. During this period, which can extend over a few years, it is important to take good care of your plant. It can seem a bit tedious, but a good start in life (see Some simple tips when planting shrubs, page 23) will definitely mean the plant is better armed against attacks of all kinds.

Even when your shrub is growing well, it is still important to remain vigilant and observant. The risk of attack by pests and diseases is already high, but climate change makes it greater still with each passing year. Below are described the most common problems affecting shrubs.

PESTS

Aphids
Aphids (aka greenfly, blackfly or plant lice) are minute, sap-sucking insects, yet they can often be spotted by the naked eye. They colonize the stems and the undersides of leaves. Some aphids attack the roots. Almost any plants can be affected. Because aphids excrete honeydew, the leaves of affected plants are sticky, curled or distorted. Ants, which collect the honeydew, can been seen on the plant as well. When possible, try to remove aphids by hand, squashing them between your finger and thumb. Also, encourage natural predators such as ladybirds and lacewings into the garden. Organic sprays are available, too. Avoid the use of synthetic insecticides if possible.

In order to protect bees and other pollinating insects, never spray shrubs when they are in flower.

Sawfly larvae
Creamy white, caterpillar-like larvae with tiny black spots, black heads and orange stains feed on the leaves of shrubs such as barberry (*Berberis*) and mahonia and can cause severe defoliation. In fact, only these larvae can cause such devastation to these shrubs. The safest, wildlife-friendly way to

OPPOSITE TOP Blackflies can be found on many garden plants during spring and summer.
OPPOSITE BOTTOM When sawfly larvae eat plant leaves they cause unsightly damage, and can even kill the plant.

The box tree caterpillar feeds on box bushes and causes devastation in a very short time.

Scale insects (top) and vine weevil (above) can be killed by introducing biological control such as nematodes.

get rid of sawfly larvae is manual control. From spring onwards, check the shrubs regularly and remove the larvae by hand. Dispose of them in a bucket full of water so that they drown. Avoid using pesticides, which can harm natural predators such as birds and ground beetles. If hand-picking is not possible, organic contact insecticides can be used but only in the most careful way as they are dangerous to bees and other pollinating insects.

Box tree caterpillar
These voracious caterpillars are, in fact, the larvae of a moth. They are greenish yellow with black heads, and thick-black and thin-white stripes along the length of eac body. They produce a white webbing over their feeding area, and a great amount of pale yellow droppings. Box tree caterpillars devour box (*Buxus*) leaves in record time. They can destroy a medium-sized shrub within a week. From spring to autumn, check your shrub regularly for signs of the pest. Once spotted, remove the caterpillars by hand, without forgetting the ones that are deep inside the shrub. Repeat the operation every day. It can be a fastidious and unpleasant job. Unfortunately, chemical controls have to be avoided as they will kill other insects. For peace of mind and less manual intervention, planting an alternative to box such as Japanese holly (*Ilex crenata*; see page 86) has become increasingly popular – and, for now, the caterpillars don't like it.

Scale insects

These sap-sucking insects, 1–10mm/ $\frac{1}{20}$–$\frac{1}{2}$in in diameter, are covered in waxy shells and so look like little bumps on stems and the undersides of leaves, which may be sticky and blackened with sooty mould, caused by a non-parasitic fungus. To minimize infestations by scale insects, encourage natural predators such as ladybirds in the garden. Some birds will eat scale insects. Biological control agents like nematodes can be applied; these microscopic parasites hunt, penetrate and destroy the scale insects, but do not prey on ladybirds, earthworms or most other beneficial insects. Organic sprays containing natural pyrethrum are also available.

Vine weevil

The adult black beetles are 9mm/ $\frac{1}{2}$in long, with yellow stains on their wings, while the recognizable 'C'-shaped, creamy white larvae are about 10mm/ $\frac{1}{2}$in long and have brown heads. Both adults and larvae feed on a wide range of shrubs. In spring and summer, the adults eat the leaves, and in autumn and winter the larvae eat the shrub roots. These attacks wreak havoc on plants growing in pots. You will realize you have vine weevils when you notice irregular notches from the edges of the leaves in summer. In autumn and winter, a healthy-looking shrub will suddenly wilt and die because all its roots have been devoured by vine weevil grubs. To get rid of the adults, pick them up at night, using a torchlight and your fingers; you will not find any vine weevils during daytime. To get rid of the larvae, introduce biological control agents like vine weevil nematodes in late summer, when the soil is warm and moist.

DISEASES

Box blight

This devastating fungal infection attacks the leaves and stems of common box (*Buxus sempervirens*), and spreads rapidly in warm humid weather. The symptoms are leaves turning brown and falling, resulting in bare patches, and black streaks developing on young stems. In wet conditions, white spores may be seen on the undersides of infected leaves. As soon as you spot signs of infection, cut out the affected parts of the plant (do so only in dry weather) and remove fallen leaves from within and around the plant. If the shrub is badly infected, cut it back by half or even right back almost to ground level. Box blight doesn't attack roots so the shrub may sprout again. In a worst-case scenario, remove the plant completely. Dispose of infected materials with your non-recycling waste. Always clean your hands, shoes and tools with disinfectant afterwards.

Fireblight

Fireblight is a bacterial disease that affects shrubs of the Rosaceae family such as cotoneasters, Christmas berry (*Photinia*) and firethorn (*Pyracantha*). The leaves turn blackish brown, shrivel and die, but they remain clinging to the stem. Blossoms wilt and die. At the first signs of fireblight, immediately remove all affected parts of the plant. Dispose of infected plant material in a bin bag with your non-recycling house waste. Do not put such material into your compost bin. Disinfect your pruning tools thoroughly before reusing them for another task.

OPPOSITE TOP Box blight is a fungal infection causing considerable damage to box (*Buxus*), especially in wet and warm weather.
OPPOSITE BOTTOM Fireblight is a disease caused by *Erwinia amylovora* bacterium.

ABOVE *Armillaria* is a genus of parasitic fungi that includes *A. mellea* (known as honey fungi), which live on trees and woody shrubs.
RIGHT Forsythia gall produces a brown, irregular, thick swelling on a plant stem.

Forsythia gall

This disease may be caused by a fungus or a bacteria. The symptoms are easy to spot. A light brown growth looking like a thick clump of firm flower buds appears on a stem, individually or in a group. While forsythia gall is most visible during the winter months when the stems are leafless, it can appear in any season. Over time, this can cause wilting, stem dieback and eventually, in severe cases, shrub death. There is no treatments available to kill the disease so the best thing to do is to cut off the affected stems either at their point of origin or 10–15cm/4–6in below each gall formation, leaving the rest of the stem intact. Always clean and disinfect your secateurs or pruning shears afterwards. Dispose of the diseased stems with your non-recycling waste.

Honey fungus

This terrible disease is caused by the fungus *Armillaria*. It spreads underground, attacking and killing the roots of woody and perennial plants. Upper parts of the affected plant die suddenly, leaves appear smaller and paler, there are no flowers, and the bark bleeds and cracks. The plant lacks vigour and dies. The fungus itself is sometimes hard to spot. Creamy white mycelium growing under the bark at the base of the trunk is a sign of infection. In autumn, clusters of mushrooms may appear above ground – their colour varying between an orange-yellow honey to different shades of brown. There are no chemical controls for honey fungus at present. The only solution is to dig out the affected plant, including the stump and all the roots. The infected material should then be burnt or taken to landfill.

Phytophthora root rot

Microscopic, fungus-like organisms cause *Phytophthora* root rot. They are found in poorly drained soil, where they patiently wait for a host plant. Above ground, the leaves of the affected plants wilt, fade to yellow long before autumn sets in, and the branches die. Step by step, things get worse until the plant dies. Once you have removed your dead plant, you can see its poor root system with many of the smallest roots rotten. There is no treatment for *Phytophthora* root rot, but prevention helps. It is essential not to plant in waterlogged soil – all shrubs in this book needing free-draining soils. Do not hesitate to improve the soil drainage, if necessary, by adding horticultural grit.

Powdery mildew

This fungal disease affects the foliage of shrubs such as viburnum and rhododendron. The infection becomes visible in spring, when a white dusty growth covers the upper and lower surfaces of leaves, as if they have been coated in talcum powder. Powdery mildew occurs when air circulation around a plant is poor and when humidity levels are too high. Therefore, prune your shrub to open its structure and cut out branches that are touching nearby plants so that the air can circulate better inside and around each one, and humidity levels are also reduced. Water your shrub regularly during periods of drought.

ENVIRONMENTAL PROBLEMS

Drought

Lack of water for a prolonged period causes leaves to wilt, scorch and drop. In the long term, even after it starts raining again, a shrub can still suffer from the effects of drought: growth is slower, branches are dying back and the entire plant eventually dies. The best remedy is to choose drought-resistant plants in a hot climate or where there is dry soil. Mediterranean plants, for example, can survive for months without a drop of water. Applying a thick layer of mulch over the soil will help retain the precious moisture, while watering at night will reduce evaporation.

Frost and wind

Hardiness is a very important factor to consider when choosing the right shrub for your garden, otherwise your plant may die of cold after its first winter outdoor (see Hardiness ratings, page 15). Against unexpected cold weather, protecting the plant and its roots is sometimes enough. Tender plants in pots should overwinter in a greenhouse or indoors.

Strong winds can break branches and uproot shrubs, leaving them more vulnerable to further damage from pests (see page 130) and diseases (see page 133). Constant wind pulls moisture from the leaves causing them to wilt and brown. Therefore, use fences, wind-tolerant shrubs and other windbreaks to provide good protection against the negative effects of wind.

Environmental stress such as a long period of frosts or drought can kill an entire plant.

Camellias are typical of early-spring flowering shrubs whose blossoms are prone to damage after severe frost.

Nutrient deficiency

Symptoms of nutrient deficiencies on shrubs are smaller, yellow or reddish leaves, slow growth and poor flowering. The reason for these can be that the soil lacks nutrients and therefore cannot pass them to the plant. The plant itself can suffer deficiencies if it cannot take up the nutrients present in the soil. Particularly vulnerable are shrubs growing in soils that are very acidic, very alkaline, waterlogged or desiccated. For every deficiency (of nitrogen, potassium, phosphorus, magnesium or iron), fertilizers are widely available (see also Fertilizers, page 27). As a preventive measure against nutrient problems, apply a 10–15cm/ 4–6in layer of organic farmyard manure around the base of your shrub every spring.

Physical damage

Wounds caused by bad pruning cuts (jagged cuts or cuts in the wrong place) allow diseases to enter the shrub more easily. Pruning too much can be as bad – or even worse – than not pruning at all. The stress that is put on a plant by over-pruning makes it weaker and less resistant to pests and diseases. The damage cannot always be fixed and, with time, the shrub will die. Pruning at the wrong time of the year may cause the plant to bleed sap, which also makes it more vulnerable. See also Pruning, page 28.

What to do when

Most shrubs can grow happily without regular maintenance. However, they can quickly become overgrown, overcrowded and no longer suitable for your garden. To get the best out of your shrubs year after year, you need to give them routine care in the appropriate seasons.

SPRING

- Plant container-grown deciduous hedges and shrubs (see Planting a pot-grown shrub in the ground, page 104).
- Plant evergreen and half-hardy shrubs once there is little risk of frost (see Some simple tips when planting shrubs, page 23).
- Hard prune shrubs such as dogwood (*Cornus*) and smoke tree (*Cotinus*) down to the base, to encourage new growth (see Hard pruning, page 30).
- Clip evergreen hedges (see Hedge pruning, page 31).
- Prune evergreen shrubs just before new growth starts (see Pruning: Evergreen shrubs, page 29). Apply a 10–15cm/4–6in layer of organic farmyard manure afterwards.
- Mulch each border with a 10–15cm/ 4–6in layer of organic farmyard manure or soil conditioner. Work spent mushroom compost into heavy clay soil, to break it up.
- Keep borders and beds free of weeds.
- Remove the top 10cm/4in of soil in

pots and replace it with new potting compost mixed with controlled-released fertilizer (see Looking after shrubs in containers, page 25). Water well afterwards.
- Check for box tree caterpillars (see page 132), sawfly larvae (see page 130) and aphids (see page 130).
- Apply biological control, such as nematodes in the early hours of the day or at dusk as they are sensitive to light (see Scale insects, page 133, and Vine weevils, page 133).
- Once the weather warms up, harden off cuttings by placing them outdoors during the day or in a cold frame (see Hardening off, page 32). After a couple of weeks, they can be planted out, provided that there is minimal risk of frost.
- Take softwood cuttings (see page 31).
- Propagate evergreen and some deciduous shrubs by layering (see Simple layering, page 35).
- Pick elder (*Sambucus*) flowers for cordial preparation (see Home-made elderflower cordial, page 118).
- Prune early-spring-flowering shrubs once they have finished flowering (see Flowering shrubs, page 29).

SUMMER

- Take the last softwood cuttings (see page 31).

Weeding is a year-round gardening activity, except during spells of snow and ice.

- Water recently planted shrubs and non-drought-tolerant ones, making sure that the soil doesn't dry out for too long (see Watering, page 24).
- Keep beds and borders free of weeds.
- Mulch if the weather is very dry in order to retain moisture (see Mulching, page 24).
- Remove suckers as soon as they appear (see page 27).
- Transplant cuttings into individual pots, as they take root.
- Prune early-summer-flowering shrubs immediately after they have finished flowering (see Flowering shrubs, page 29.
- Feed camellias and rhododendrons with a controlled-release ericaceous fertilizer at the rate recommended by the manufacturer. Water them well in dry weather.
- Clip evergreen hedges such as box (*Buxus*) and Wilson's honeysuckle (*Lonicera ligustrina* var. *yunnanensis*) if needed (see Hedge pruning, page 31). Remove all the box clippings afterwards, to minimize the spread of box blight (see page 133).
- Check for pests and diseases: powdery mildew (see page 136), box blight (see page 133), box tree caterpillars (see page 132), sawfly larvae (see page 130), and aphids (see page 130). Apply biological control for vine weevil (see page 133), especially in your pots.

- Trim lavender (*Lavandula*) immediately after flowering (see page 90). Keep the faded flowers for making dried lavender bags (see page 88).
- Take semi-ripe cuttings from evergreen shrubs such as barberry (*Berberis*), Mexican orange blossom (*Choisya*) and lavender (*Lavandula*). (See Semi-ripe cuttings, page 32.)

AUTUMN

- Keep beds and borders free of weeds.
- In early autumn, there is still time to apply biological control for vine weevil if the soil is warm and moist.
- Plant pot-grown shrubs in the garden (see Some simple tips when planting shrubs, page 23) and hedging plants (see Planting a hedge, page 126).
- Water newly planted shrubs if the weather is dry (see Watering, page 24).
- Check for honey fungus (see page 135).
- Tidy up box (*Buxus*) hedges for a crisp finish over winter. Remove all the clippings immediately.
- Collect fallen leaves and make a leafmould pile. Most leaves take about two years to break down.
- Take the last semi-ripe cuttings (see page 32).
- Start taking hardwood cuttings (see page 34).
- Propagate deciduous shrubs such as camellia, dogwood (*Cornus*), witch hazel (*Hamamelis*) and lilac (*Syringa*) by simple layering (see page 35).
- Order bare-root plants as they are now available.

WINTER

- Plant bare-root deciduous shrubs and hedging plants, assuming that the ground is not frozen (see Some simple tips when planting shrubs, page 23), and Planting a hedge, page 126).
- Protect newly planted hedges and half-hardy shrubs from cold winds and frosts by applying a thick layer of mulch around the base of each plant (see Mulching, page 24).
- Wrap single specimen shrubs in horticultural fleece (see Winter protection, page 25).
- Overwinter tender and half-hardy shrubs in pots indoors, to protect them from frosts.
- Remove any snow sitting on shrub branches.
- Firm back newly planted shrubs if they have been lifted by frost or strong winds.
- Keep beds and borders free of weeds.
- Clean tools and sharpen cutting blades.
- Take hardwood cuttings from deciduous shrubs such as forsythia (see Hardwood cuttings, page 34).
- Renovate/hard prune overgrown deciduous shrubs and hedges. Mulch and feed afterwards (see Hard pruning, page 30).
- Visit public gardens for winter planting ideas.
- Prune late summer- and autumn-flowering shrubs (see Pruning, page 28). Mulch generously afterwards.
- Prune winter-flowering shrubs once they have finished flowering (see Pruning, page 28). Mulch generously afterwards.

OPPOSITE TOP AND BOTTOM Autumn is the right time to start a leafmould pile by collecting fallen leaves, while winter can be spent cleaning and sharpening tools.

Index

Quarto

First published in 2023 by Frances Lincoln,
an imprint of Quarto.
One Triptych Place,
London, SE1 9SH
United Kingdom
T (0)20 7700 6700 F (0)20 7700 8066
www.Quarto.com

ISBN 978-0-7112-8241-4
eISBN 978-0-7112-8242-1

10 9 8 7 6 5 4 3 2 1

Typeset in Adobe Garamond and
Neue Haas Grotesk Display
Design by Glenn Howard

Printed in China

Photographic acknowledgments

Alamy: 21 (Ozgur Coskun), 33 above (BIOSPHOTO), 63 (Alex Ramsay), 134 above (David Humphreys),

Valerie Boujard: 2, 9, 10 above, 12, 13, 43, 49, 57, 64, 65, 73, 83, 89, 96, 97, 105, 112, 113, 119, 127,

GAP Photos: 135 right (Geoff Kidd)

Shutterstock: 6–7 (Maria Evseyeva), 10 below (Maren Winter), 14 (1000 Words), 16 above (Peter Turner Photography), 16 below (Besjunior), 18 (Suti Stock Photo), 19 (Jacquie Klose), 22 (VH-studio), 25 (Miriam Doerr/Martin Frommherz), 26 (Ingrid Balabanova), 28 (YuliaDerid), 29 (Georgy Dzyura), 30 (Cuhle-Fotos), 33 below (Radovan1), 34 (Mariia Boiko), 36–7 (Federico Magonio), 38 (Skyprayer2005), 40 (Maria Evseyeva), 41 (Olga S photography), 44 (Aleksandra Duda), 45 (Alexander Denisenko), 46 (Lois GoBe), 47 (Nick Pecker), 50 (Peter Turner Photography), 51 (Alex Manders), 52 (nnattalli), 54 (Peter Turner Photography), 55 (Kathrine Andi), 58 (SakSa), 59 (Lagutkin Alexey), 60 (Peter Turner Photography), 61 (shepherdsatellite), 66 (InfoFlowersPlants), 67 (Tom McPherson), 68 (Marc ANSEL), 69 (mizy), 70 (Nahhana), 71 (Nick Pecker), 75 (Ihor Hvozdetskyi), 77 (Tony Baggett), 79 (Josie Elias), 86 (Danny Hummel), 87 (Orest Iyzhechka), 91 (patjo), 94 (Joe Kuis), 95 (Bildagentur Zoonar GmbH), 100 (Tom Meaker), 101 (Manfred Ruckszio), 103 (Sheryl Watson), 106 (Peter Turner Photography), 107 (aniana), 110 (Nahhana), 117 (nnattalli), 120 (Kuttelvaserova Stuchelova), 124 (prambuwesas), 125 (Edita Medeina), 129 (APugach), 131 above (Andrii Medvediuk), 131 below (Aprilflower), 132 left (Tomasash), 132 right above (Young Swee Ming), 132 right below (Lutsenko_Oleksandr), 134 below (Olya Maximenko), 135 left (akslocum), 137 left (Anna Sadovskaia), 137 right (AnnaNel), 139 David Prahl

Author's acknolwedgments

I could never have written this book on my own. Thanks to Helena Dove who started it all, to Pei Chu, Lydia White and Gina Fullerlove, to Hattie Moore, to Joanna Chisholm. An even bigger thank you to my daughters Salomé, Capucine and Candice Savary for supporting a mother who talks only about plants, and to my husband Clovis Krieger, who introduced me to the world of gardens more than ten years ago and who spent a lot of time in the kitchen while I was working on this book.